Maritime Heritage

CROSSING THE CHANNEL

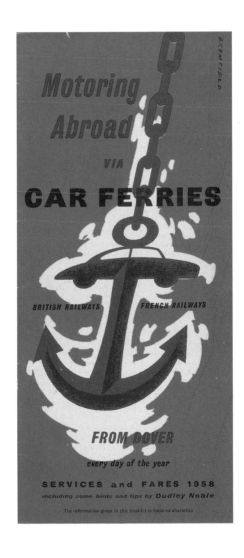

Above left Part of the vast car-ferry complex in Dover's Eastern Docks. The elevated roadway (centre) separates arriving from departing traffic, while the tall brick building (left) houses administration offices and Dover Port Control. Alongside this office block, in darker brick, is the original 1953 terminal building. The curved front at ground level was the café and waiting room. Facilities for departing passengers are now located much further to the right of the picture, adjacent to the present-day ferry berths.

Left Dover's Western Docks, with a ferry passing into the harbour through the Western Entrance. Curving round on the right and forming the Western Arm of the harbour is the Admiralty Pier. The white building on the right is the former Lord Warden Hotel, and behind it is the harbour station, originally called Dover Marine, but now closed and converted into a cruise-ship terminal. The structure connected by a walk-way to the station is the floating Jetfoil terminal, which was later moved to Ramsgate. To the left of this is the site of the old train-ferry terminal. Dover Hoverport, with three craft on the apron, can be seen on the left. This was built adjacent to the Prince of Wales Pier, visited in the early years of the century by transatlantic liners en route from Antwerp and Hamburg to America. Below the Hoverport is the Tidal Basin and the enclosed Granville Dock, which opened in 1874.

Above Looking out over Dover Harbour across the Channel, with the never-ending procession of ferries entering and leaving. Further out, shipping passes down the Channel in the westbound separation lane. Eastbound Channel traffic must pass closer to the French side. The coast of France, with the cliffs of Cap Blanc-Nez and Cap Gris-Nez, can be seen in the distance. Ferry traffic from Dover to Calais (which is situated to the left of this picture and is visible from Dover on a clear day) must alter course to cross the Channel separation lanes at right-angles.

of all aspects of foreign travel, were common. For many years, even after the last war, it was still the practice for every passenger to be individually interrogated on arrival in Britain by a Customs Officer, who would often ask for personal baggage to be opened and for packages to be unwrapped, making every incoming traveller feel like a prospective criminal. The interest then was in intercepting the illicit bottle of French perfume, a smuggled Swiss watch, or the odd half-litre of spirits above the duty-free limit, rather than in the more sinister trade in drugs or the equipment of terrorism that is the chief concern today.

It is only quite recently that the notion that a ferry crossing might actually be an opportunity to be enjoyed, rather than just a means of transport, has been exploited by the shipping operators. Now, talk of 'cruising across' and descriptions of on-board gastronomic delights and other distractions are commonplace in ferry brochures, although much of this has been due to the rising pressures of competition. This competition, too, has changed the face of cross-Channel operations more rapidly over the last few decades than ever before. None of the current 'big five' ferry names - Brittany, Hoverspeed, P&O, Sally and Stena - were major players in the Channel trade as recently as 20 years ago. Other once familiar names, such as Townsend, Thoresen, Normandy and Sealink, have come and gone. Yet today's operators are inheritors of a system of cross-Channel routes that really began to develop with the coming of steam.

2. THE AGE OF STEAM

The development of the Channel ports and the ferry services that have operated from them is closely linked to the growth of the railways, although today it is connections with the motorway network that are usually more important. Until the railways arrived, the short-sea cross-Channel routes were competing with the direct but longer services running to the Continent from London. These were operated by ships such as those of the General Steam Navigation Company. There is a thread of continuity here, since the GSNC was absorbed, much later, into the vast P&O Group, which is now a major operator of Channel ferries. It was also the GSNC that ran the well-known Eagle pleasure steamers that plied between London's Tower Pier and the Estuary towns, with occasional trips across to the French coast. Sadly, these services ended in the 1970s.

It was not in Britain, however, but in Belgium that the railway first reached the Channel coast when, in 1838, the line linking Brussels with Ostend was completed. This line was extended to Liège in 1843, and the following year reached the Prussian frontier at Herbesthal, where it connected with the Rheinische Eisenbahn running to Cologne and beyond. The Belgian State Railways were developed rapidly under the auspices of King Leopold I, and a regular steamer service from Ostend to Dover was started by the Belgian Government in 1846.

The first railway line in Britain to the South Coast was opened by the London & Southampton Railway (later to become the London & South Western) in 1840. It ran from a London terminus at Nine Elms (a few miles down the line from the present Waterloo) to Southampton, from where a regular packet-boat service was already operating to Le Havre. From Le Havre the road journey on to Paris, broadly following the course of the River Seine, was a relatively straightforward one, even in the days of horse-drawn vehicles. This route was in fact mentioned by Charles Dickens in his novel *Dombey and Son*.

Le Havre is closer to Paris than the more northerly ports of Boulogne or Calais, but the sea passage from England is a long one. It was the short-sea routes from Kent that would benefit most from being connected to the railway system, but early plans to build a direct line from London to Dover were thwarted by unco-operative landowners who did not welcome the prospect of their farms, hop-fields and orchards being bisected by the tracks of the smoke-belching iron monster.

In 1843 the South Eastern Railway (SER) reached Folkestone from London Bridge, the first railway terminal to be built in London. The line was then continued along the edge of the sea, beneath the Warren and Shakespeare Cliff, to reach Dover the following year. Its route from London was, however, a rather circuitous one, branching off the London to Brighton line at Redhill station (then called Reigate), and continuing, via Tonbridge and Ashford, to Folkestone.

The harbour at Folkestone was at that time in a very run-down state, but it was purchased from the Government by the SER, who constructed a steep railway line down from the town to the shore, and developed the harbour as its base for a new cross-Channel steamer service to Boulogne and Calais. The railways were initially prohibited from operating shipping services themselves, and therefore did so through associated companies, but this restriction was relaxed from 1862.

The people of Dover, whose town had been the principal port of embarkation for the Continent for centuries, were decidedly unhappy at these developments at nearby Folkestone. Not only did they find themselves at the end of what was a virtual branch line, rather than having their own direct rail-link with London, but they also risked losing much of their cross-Channel business to Folkestone.

Not everyone, however, shared their view. *The Railway Times* believed that Dover had abused its monopoly position, and stated bluntly:

> 'The Dover people are loud in their complaints at the establishment of Folkestone Harbour. The little town of Folkestone is beginning to rival them, and they are miserably jealous.'

The Nord Railway in France opened its line from Paris to Boulogne in 1848, and reached Calais and Dunkirk, by way of a longer route through Lille, the following year. It was still easier, however, for passengers arriving at Calais to take the horse-drawn diligence to Boulogne, and connect with the railway there.

Train services connecting with the steamer sailings between Folkestone and Boulogne were now being operated on both sides of the Channel, linking London Bridge station with the Gare du Nord in Paris. The total journey time between the two capitals was less than 11 hours; before the advent of the railways it would have taken anything from three days to a week.

Dover lobbied hard for a more direct link with London, and eventually the East Kent Railway, which had been building a local line to serve North and East Kent, won parliamentary approval to build a railway line from Faversham, via Canterbury, to Dover, and renamed itself the London, Chatham & Dover Railway (LC&DR). The

The through connection from London to Paris offered by the London & South Western Railway, and using the company's 1894-built steamers *Alma* and *Columbia* between Southampton and Le Havre, provided passengers with an overnight crossing of the Channel in finely appointed vessels that were superior to those then operating on the short-sea routes from Dover and Folkestone. Both were twin-screw ships, unlike those on the more easterly routes where paddle steamers were still employed on cross-Channel services because of the limited depth of water available in the harbours. Being specifically designed for night sailings, the L&SWR ships were well-equipped with comfortable cabin accommodation. The evening boat-train from Waterloo ran directly into the docks at Southampton and alongside the quay. A few years later a similar system of direct transfer between ship and train was introduced at Le Havre, where previously passengers needed to be conveyed by omnibus from the harbour to the town station.

company's new London terminus was Victoria, which it shared with the Brighton line. Victoria Station opened in 1860, and was named, not directly after the Queen, but after the street in which it is built. The entire line to the coast, with a station at Dover Town (later renamed Dover Priory) and a temporary station at Dover harbour, was completed in 1861.

With this new line in operation, the Chatham railway company began its own steamer services from Dover, and a period of great rivalry commenced between this company and the South Eastern. Both operated competing boat services to France, the SER from Dover and Folkestone to Boulogne, and the LC&DR between Dover and Calais. From 1864 the two companies shared the use of the same harbour station at Dover, an exposed, windswept affair situated at the shore end of the Admiralty Pier.

In 1867, in France, a more direct railway line to Calais was opened, running along the coast from Boulogne. Following this, the Dover-Calais route, with its rather shorter passage, began to become more popular. The trade war on the short-sea crossings intensified further in 1868, when the SER completed its own direct line to the Channel coast of Kent, by way of Sevenoaks and Tonbridge, from a new West End terminus at Charing Cross. Rival boat-trains connecting with cross-Channel sailings then ran from both Charing Cross and Victoria.

Both railway companies maintained a reasonably reliable cross-Channel service, but because of the restricted depths of water available at the ports, sailings were governed by tidal conditions. The ships were sturdy but small, yet even so tenders were sometimes needed to disembark passengers (for which a large toll was usually extracted by the local boatmen) when, at low tide, the steamers were unable to reach the quay.

Development of the harbours, including the deepening of access channels, the construction of harbour walls and the building of dockside facilities, was carried out in a piecemeal fashion, as funds could be raised and expenditure justified. The massive harbour that one can now see at Dover, however, and which was completed in 1909 by enclosing the whole of Dover Bay with three huge breakwaters, was not the result of commercial enterprise, but of the long-standing desire of successive governments to build, for naval purposes, a 'national harbour of refuge' on the Eastern Channel, a role that it has never fulfilled.

The original East Kent line of the Chatham railway continued eastwards from Faversham, through a new town

that it developed at Herne Bay, and on to Thanet, the eastern tip of Kent, which had been an island until the 16th century. The line ended at Ramsgate, where it tunnelled through the cliffs to a station on the beach, close to Ramsgate Pier. This station opened in 1863 and was in use for 60 years, until it was eventually closed in 1923. It had been the Government's intention to develop Ramsgate as a packet port, but disputes with the Admiralty and the poor financial state of the railway company resulted in this scheme being abandoned. Ramsgate had to wait until the 1980s before it was to become an important cross-Channel port.

Other schemes that came to nought included a plan, proposed during the 1870s, to build a cross-Channel harbour at Dungeness, near the Kentish border with Sussex. Here there is deep water close to the shore, but the Government's desire to develop Dover put an end to this proposal. At Christchurch, close to Bournemouth, there had been a plan by the Wimborne & Christchurch Railway to embark upon an extensive development of the harbour and to operate a ferry service to Cherbourg from a berth close to Hengistbury Head. There was, however, little enthusiasm for this scheme and it was soon abandoned.

Meanwhile, the London to Brighton line of the London,

MARITIME HERITAGE

Left Berths 5 and 6 at Dover's Eastern Docks, showing the three-level loading ramps. In this 1985 view coaches are disembarking from a Townsend Thoresen vessel, which has just arrived from Calais. The upper enclosed ramp is for foot-passengers, who are conveyed through the terminal area by bus. To the right, a British Railways Sealink ship is waiting to load for Boulogne, while on the extreme left is a Belgian ferry recently arrived from Ostend. Alongside the Eastern Arm at the top left of the picture is a reefer ship (fruit carrier), demonstrating that the Port of Dover handles a considerable amount of conventional cargo arriving from far beyond the confines of the Channel, in addition to its better-known cross-Channel traffic.

Below left Victoria station in London, photographed in 1975, which for over 75 years from the end of the First World War until the 1990s was the traditional 'Gateway to the Continent', with regular boat-train services connecting with the Channel ports. The journalist and author H. V. Morton wrote of his occasional visits to Victoria during the 1930s where he would purchase a one-penny platform ticket simply to watch the hustle of activity here and observe with fascination the interesting assortment of people as they boarded the morning departures for the Continent.

Brighton & South Coast Railway, which had opened in 1841, was extended to Lewes and Newhaven in 1847. Newhaven was already in use as a cross-Channel port, but the service to Dieppe was very uncomfortable and unreliable. In France, a branch line to Dieppe from the Paris-Rouen main line had been completed in 1846 by the Ouest Railway. With the arrival of train services on both sides of the Channel, more regular sailings commenced between the two ports. These were run jointly by the Brighton company and the Société de Chemin de Fer de L'Ouest, with the revenues being split in the ratio 37/56ths to France and 19/56ths to Britain. This curious arrangement, which continued until joint operation on this route ceased in 1985, was based on the length of the rail journeys from the ports to the respective capitals.

Although it is a longer sea crossing to France than from ports in Kent, a glance at a map will show that the Newhaven-Dieppe route is the most direct between London and Paris, and it therefore provided the cheapest (though far from quickest) link between these two cities. While Folkestone and Dover were able to cream off most of the 1st Class traffic between Britain and France, the Newhaven-Dieppe route developed into an important connection for cheaper-class travel. One commentator on this 'economy service' in the early days, however, stated that:

'. . . the fares being much cheaper than by the South Eastern route, the boats were crowded and the miseries endured by deck passengers were very great; they were often landed more like drowned rats than human beings.'

It is perhaps surprising that it was Newhaven, rather than Shoreham, that became the cross-Channel port of Sussex. Shoreham had a superior harbour that was less prone to silting-up than Newhaven. It was closer to Brighton and had better rail connections with London. Although it had been the original plan to base services at Shoreham, the harbour authorities there were not enthusiastic about this trade (a decision they may well have regretted later), and one can only speculate as to how things might otherwise have developed had they taken a different view.

Further west, in Dorset, Weymouth had been an impor-tant link for trade with the Channel Islands since the Middle Ages, and in 1794 it became the official Post Office packet station for mails and passengers. The arrival of the railway at Southampton in 1840, however, allowed the larger port to capture and develop much of this trade. The railway reached Weymouth in 1857, but it was only when the Great Western Railway began its own steamer services from Weymouth in 1889 that the Dorset port regained something of its former importance.

In France, the Western group of railways had spread from St Lazare station, in Paris, to reach Le Havre in 1847, and Cherbourg in 1858, where the new line was officially opened by Queen Victoria. The port of Le Havre, situated at the mouth of the River Seine, had been established in the 16th century for naval purposes, and soon attained considerable importance, also attracting commercial traffic.

Cherbourg, strategically positioned at the end of the Contentin peninsula jutting out into the Channel, had long been a natural port for travellers between England and Normandy, and for over a century had been under English control and the occasional residence of King Henry II. The enormous outer harbour was constructed, like Dover's, for military purposes. Started by Louis XVI, it was not finally completed until the time of Napoleon III. Both Cherbourg and Le Havre developed as important terminals for the transatlantic trade, and through them passed many thousands of emigrants from Central Europe, bound for a new life in the United States.

With the extension of the railways, the speed and convenience of Continental travel were considerably improved, and possibilities for journeying much further afield were opened up. The Paris-Strasbourg line was opened in 1852, linking with the Strasbourg-Basle railway and so providing direct rail connections from the Channel coast to Switzerland. The Paris-Lyons line was extended to reach the Mediterranean at Marseilles in 1855; it continued along the coast as far as Nice in 1862, and to the Italian frontier in 1864. By 1866 one could travel by train, with appropriate changes and overnight stops, all the way from Calais to the South of Italy. There was a continuous rail link eastwards to Moscow, and another stretching south-west through Spain, to Madrid, Seville and Lisbon. Within a period of just 20 years, therefore, journeys across Europe, which would have been long and arduous, or would have necessitated a long sea voyage, had been transformed by the power of steam.

The package tour industry, which introduced foreign travel to those who might never have had the courage to undertake such ventures unaided, began during the middle of the 19th century. It was started by one man, a craftsman and part-time Baptist preacher from Market Harborough in Leicestershire. An enthusiastic young lady who joined one of his early tours to Switzerland wrote:

'It really is a miracle. Everything is organised, everything is catered for, one does not have to bother oneself with anything at all, neither timings, nor luggage, nor hotels. And, do you know, I have met the man who arranges it all. I have said "Good morning" to him. He is named Mister Cook and they say he is a Saint.'

Thomas Cook first took a party to the Continent in 1855, although he had some trouble in persuading the railway companies to grant him discounted fares. Soon, however, the benefits of mass travel became obvious to the operators, and Cook was able to obtain the lowest ever cross-Channel fare - £1 3rd Class return from London to Paris. Not everyone, though, shared this enthusiasm. He was accused of turning what had been an adventure into an institution. Long-term British residents in Switzerland and the French Riviera were appalled at this influx into their idyllic retreats of large numbers of their fellow countrymen. But the travel business that Thomas Cook started also catered for the independent traveller, and the network of booking agencies that he established provided much of the trade on which the ferry operators depended. But in spite of this growth in tourism, the Channel crossing unfortunately often left much to be desired.

The novelist Charles Dickens travelled widely, and crossed both the Channel and the Atlantic several times, although he seldom had a good word to say about the experience. In his *The Uncommercial Traveller* he describes his impressions of a night crossing from Dover to Calais in the 1860s:

> 'The wind blows stiffly from the Nor'East, the sea runs high, we ship a deal of water, the night is dark and cold, and the shapeless passengers lie about in melancholy bundles as if they were sorted out for the laundress.'

Much of the deck space on board the steamers was exposed to the elements, and although there were proposals to provide more closed-in protection, this was resisted by shipowners who considered that the stability of the vessels might be affected by this. Said one spokesman, 'In the thirty years that the Company had navigated the Channel they had never lost a passenger. It was better for people to get wet than drowned.'

Nevertheless, schemes were adopted to try to improve the lot of the hapless passenger. In 1872 the SER had the decks of its steamer *Albert Edward* covered in. The decks were drier in a rough sea, but her speed was found to be reduced by these changes.

Three rather more unorthodox vessels were also built as an experiment. The *Castalia* was introduced on the Dover-Calais run in 1874 by the English Channel Steamship Company. She was designed like a catamaran, having two half-hulls with a platform-deck mounted between them and paddle wheels beneath. She was, however, slow and often late, and as she was not operated by the railway companies the boat-trains never waited for her. The second strange ship was the *Bessemer*, built for the Chatham railway, also in 1874. She had the ultimate in innovation, a swaying saloon, mounted on gimbals and intended to counteract the motion of the vessel in a heavy sea! Hardly surprisingly, this was not a great success. She was also difficult to manoeuvre, and was scrapped three years later.

The third vessel was the *Calais-Douvres*, built in 1877 for the English Channel Steamship Company, and was a development of its earlier *Castalia*. She had two complete hulls side-by-side, and although rather slow, she continued to operate on the Channel for ten years. Following her eventual scrapping, no further unusual craft appeared until the arrival of the hovercraft in the next century.

As cross-Channel travel developed, improvements to harbour facilities were gradually introduced. In France, a new Gare Maritime (Harbour Station) was opened in 1876 on the Quai Bonaparte in Boulogne, although work on developing the harbour itself was not finished until 1885. At Calais, construction of a new harbour, together with its Gare Maritime and new hotel, was completed in 1889. In the same year improved facilities were introduced at both Newhaven and Dieppe.

As the rail network grew, so did the amenities for travelling Britons, with the development of luxurious hotels on the French Riviera and elsewhere. More long-distance railway services were introduced, but most still only operated within national borders, requiring a change of train at the frontier. A truly trans-European, international train - a luxury rail service to connect Paris with the distant Balkans - was the dream of the Belgian entrepreneur George Nagelmackers. He founded the International Sleeping-Car Company ('Wagon-Lits') and established, in 1883, the 'Express d'Orient', the 'Orient Express', the most famous of all trains that was to run right through to Istanbul, a distance of 1,400 miles. Here, close to the Golden Horn, the railway company opened its opulent Pera Palace Hotel in 1892 for the convenience of 'Orient Express' passengers. Still in business today and with much of its original interior intact, the hotel recalls an earlier, grander age of Continental travel.

A direct connection with the 'Orient Express' for travellers from Britain was later included, when a sleeping-car at the end of the early-evening boat-train from Calais to Paris ould be detached on arrival at the Gare du Nord, tru around the 'Petite Ceinture' line through the suburbs Paris, and shunted on to the 'Orient Express' waiting depart from the Gare de Lyon. Agatha Christie's f us book about this train was, in fact, originally called der on the Calais Coach.

ne of the best known of all hotels for cross-Channel vellers was Dover's popular Lord Warden Hotel, pened by the South Eastern Railway in 1853. A large, mposing square building close to the Admiralty Pier and the harbour station at the Western side of the town, it was closed in the last war. Converted into offices, it still stands today, although rather forlornly amidst the changing scene around it.

Much of the growth of the *trains de luxe* through France depended heavily on the patronage o ritish passengers. These luxurious trains reached t ir heyday between the two World Wars of the present entury, and included such famous names as e 'Calais-Mediterranean', later renamed the 'Blue Tr n'. For those travelling further afield to India and the ast, there was now the option of crossing the Channel, travelling through France by train, and boarding a P&O liner at a Mediterranean port such as Marseilles, so avoiding the long, cold and often rough passage through the Bay of Biscay. For some, therefore, the Channel crossing was just the first part of a much longer journey. Indeed, before the First World War one could purchase through tickets at London's Charing Cross station, not just to Orpington or

Above *Caledonian Princess*, completed in 1961, was the last of a long line of railway-owned steamships built by Denny Brothers of Dumbarton. Although originally based on the Irish Sea to operate a car-ferry link between Scotland and Northern Ireland, she ended her days on the Channel, operating services from Dover. She is seen here laid up in Newhaven in 1982 at the end of her career.

Right The sterns of the ferries *Vortigern*, *Normannia* and *Lord Warden*, laid up in the winter of 1970/71 in Dover's Wellington Dock to await the start of another busy summer season. Today's ferries are much too large to enter Dover's enclosed Docks, which are now used largely as a yachting marina. Furthermore, the economics of modern ferry operation demand year-round employment for the ships.

Ashford, not only to Paris, Rome or Venice, but also to Vladivostok, Nagasaki and Shanghai!

All the early steamships operating across the Channel had been paddle steamers. The first screw passenger vessels on the Channel were the *Seaford*, which ran between Newhaven and Dieppe, and the *Alma*, between Southampton and Le Havre, both introduced in 1894 and operating a fixed-schedule service that was not dependent upon the state of the tides. Paddle vessels were retained on the routes from Dover and Folkestone, however, until harbour improvements permitted deeper-draft vessels to be employed.

As passenger numbers increased, so competition grew between the various operators and national interests involved, the ships sometimes being run at a loss in an attempt to attract passengers to a particular route. The Ostend service, subsidised by the Belgian Government, was at a particular disadvantage because of its considerably longer sea crossing. Many passengers bound for Brussels travelled instead through Calais, with most of the revenue generated therefore going to France. Speed and competitive fares were thus essential for the Ostend service, and many innovations in marine engineering were first developed on this route. The *Princesse Elizabeth*, introduced in 1905 to coincide with the Liège Exhibition, was powered by Parson's steam turbines and attained a speed of 24 knots. She was the fastest ship in the world until the building of the Cunard liner *Mauretania*, and she reduced the crossing time between Ostend and Dover to just 3 hours, considerably quicker than was possible in more recent years.

The 'day-trip' market was also being developed to bring in extra income to the railway companies, by offering bargain 3rd Class fares. The result, it was said, was to bring Boulogne 'within the reach of the most jaded and impecunious of cockneys'.

The Great Exhibition in Paris, and the opening of the Eiffel Tower, took place in 1889. To cater for the expected increase in cross-Channel traffic, a new late-afternoon service to Paris was introduced, with the SER and the LC&DR both running rival, luxurious 'Club Trains' from London to connect with the steamer. These offered, for a supplementary fee, the highest standards of comfort and service. Although widely acclaimed, these trains were not a commercial success, and were abandoned four years later.

The Société de Chemin de Fer du Nord, already operating rail services in connection with cross-Channel sailings out of Calais and Boulogne, began its own steamer services from Calais to Dover in 1896, in conjunction with those of the Chatham railway. It introduced two new ships on this run, *Le Nord* and *Le Pas de Calais*, possibly the finest and certainly the largest paddle steamers ever built for service across the Channel.

In the face of continuing competition and much overlapping of services, the SER and the LC&DR finally agreed, in 1899, to amalgamate, a move that had been urged upon them for some time in the interests of both passengers and shareholders. They combined to form the South Eastern & Chatham Railway (SE&CR). By this time the Nord in France had introduced significant improvements to its boat-train services from Paris, which were now, for the first time, superior to those operating between London and the English Channel coast. The amalgamation of the two British companies allowed a long-overdue rationalisation of both train and boat services to take place, and overall improvements to be put in hand. Older vessels were withdrawn, and most boat-train services were concentrated at Charing Cross.

Significant and much-needed improvements for passengers travelling through Dover were completed in 1914, but with the outbreak of the First World War these facilities were immediately taken over for military purposes. They were finally opened for commercial traffic in 1919. These developments included new ferry berths along a widened section of the Admiralty Pier and the construction of a grand, glass-roofed railway station, Dover Marine, equipped with ornate waiting and refreshment rooms. At the time of its opening it was hailed as the finest maritime railway terminal in the world, and so it may have been. More recently, this station was renamed Dover Western Docks (perhaps by those whose sense of geography was more astute than their sense of history).

Left to gracefully decay ever since its opening 80 years before, by the time the station closed in 1994 with the ending of rail-connected sailings at Dover, most passengers passing through Dover Marine would have regarded it as the most dreary and forbidding ferry terminal imaginable. Nevertheless, it was to become listed by English Heritage as a building of exceptional historic interest. No longer used for cross-Channel sailings (or for trains), the building and its adjacent ferry berths have been redeveloped as a cruise-liner terminal for the increasing number of cruise ships that now visit Dover. The stonework has been cleaned, the glazing restored, the ironwork shot-blasted and painted in the original railway colours. New lounge areas have been built at first-floor level, directly beneath the huge glass roof. How odd it is that in the name of 'heritage', funding for such improvements can only be found after a building has ceased to serve its original purpose. Now, cruise passengers can pass through this elegant building in the fond belief that this is how it was in the grand old days of the Continental boat-trains. It wasn't!

With the opening of Dover Marine in 1919, boat-trains serving Dover and Folkestone were transferred to London's Victoria station, joining their counterparts running to Newhaven. Victoria soon became styled 'the Gateway to the Continent', serving a cosmopolitan clientele from all parts of the world in addition to the commuters of Kent and Sussex. Yet, since the earliest years of this century, through journey times by train and sea to the Continent have steadily lengthened. While the number of daily crossings of the Channel has increased enormously, later services could not match the proud claim of the South Eastern & Chatham Railway prior to 1914: 'Sea passage one hour'!

3. CAPITAL CONNECTIONS

The destination for many of those crossing the Channel from England has always been Paris. This is hardly surprising, given its proximity to Britain, its status as a major European capital, its eternal appeal as a romantic tourist city, and its position as the virtual 'hub' of the European railway network, offering onward train connections to the south, east and west. Indeed, more people travel between London and Paris than between any other two capital cities in the world. While the majority do so today by air or by tunnel, in past decades the train and the cross-Channel steamer provided the only option.

Several daily services were maintained between London and Paris. The ferries that sailed from Dover and Folkestone to Calais and Boulogne connected with railway links that ran between Victoria station, the principal London terminus for Continental boat-trains since the end of the First World War, and the Gare du Nord, in Paris. The Nord is now Europe's busiest rail terminal, a large sombre edifice built in the 1860s alongside the Rue du Faubourg-Saint-Denis, the traditional route by which the visiting English traveller would enter the city in the days before the railway.

The longer Newhaven-Dieppe crossing connected Victoria with the Ouest Railway's Gare St Lazare, a couple of kilometres west of the Nord station. This latter route has always been particularly popular with passengers travelling overnight, but it did mean arriving at Dieppe at about three in the morning, where a procession of bleary-eyed travellers could be seen heading, zombie-like, towards their waiting train for Paris. However, for economy-minded day-trippers returning, shattered, by the same route the following night, it did offer the opportunity of a bargain 15 hours in the French capital.

Overnight passengers for Paris who did not relish the thought of disembarking from their steamer in the early hours of the morning had the alternative of catching the late-evening boat-train from Waterloo, boarding the night-steamer for Le Havre at Southampton, and spending several hours in a comfortable cabin. In 1904 the travel publication *Cook's Traveller's Gazette* wondered whether 'the advantages of the London and South-Western Company's route to the Continent via Southampton and Havre are properly grasped by the tourist when mapping out his Continental holiday'. The journal heartily endorsed the company's claim to provide the most comfortable night route to the Continent, describing the finely appointed interiors of the vessels, and was at pains to point out that these were not paddle boats but twin-screw steamers. It

also commented on the charming scenery of the rail journey on both sides of the Channel. Travelling by this route, passengers could enjoy early morning tea brought to their cabin by the steward, before disembarking at Le Havre at a respectable hour. Arrival in Paris, at St Lazare, would still be by mid-morning, time enough for a quick coffee and croissant at a pavement patisserie before setting about one's business.

Paris was not the only nearby capital having regular cross-Channel connections with London. The traditional route to Brussels on both day and night services from Victoria was via Ostend. The principal sailing left Dover before midday and returned from Ostend during the afternoon, offering a journey time between London and Brussels of about 8 hours. Train services from Ostend to the Belgian capital would call at Brussels Midi before plunging beneath the centre of the city, through the underground stations of Chapelle, Brussels Central and Congres, to emerge again at Brussels Nord. There were frequent onward connections from any of the principal stations in Brussels to the Dutch capital of Amsterdam, a further 3 hours away.

The Dover-Calais route, however, offered the shortest sea crossing and provided the premier daytime connection between London and the Continent. It was the focus of many developments to improve the service and to speed up the overall journey time to the French capital. In 1926 a new luxury express train, for which a supplementary fare was payable, was introduced between Calais Maritime and the Gare du Nord, to connect with sailings from Dover. Called the 'Flèche d'Or' ('Golden Arrow'), this prestigious train brought new standards of style and comfort for 1st Class passengers.

A similar all-Pullman-car train was introduced in Britain to run between Victoria and Dover Marine. This was operated by the Southern Railway, which had been formed three years earlier through the amalgamation of the independent railway companies of southern England. The British train was not, however, named the 'Golden Arrow' until three years later. In the meantime, because of the colour scheme of the coaches, it was known informally as the 'White Pullman', although railway staff referred to it as the 'White Elephant', owing to the considerable weight of the train. Passengers could register their heavy baggage at the start of their journey and collect it on arrival in the other capital. The French authorities would examine passports and hand-luggage on the train between Calais and Paris, a common enough practice today on cross-border European rail journeys, but British

Left A 1930s travel poster depicting the Southern Railway's steamer *Canterbury* leaving Dover Harbour on the 'Golden Arrow' service to Calais. Originally carrying only 1st Class passengers when introduced in 1929 on the prestige route linking London with Paris, she was later modified for two-class operation. After the war *Canterbury* reopened the 'Golden Arrow' route in 1946, but was soon displaced by the newer and larger *Invicta*. The ship on the right of the picture is the Southern Railway's *Autocarrier*, which entered service during the same year as *Canterbury*. She was, as her name would imply, the railway company's first cross-Channel car-ferry (see Chapter 5).

Below Passengers alight from the Pullman cars of the 'Golden Arrow' at Dover Marine station on arrival from Victoria in 1967, and pass through the terminal building to board their waiting ship. The ornate lamps and starched table-cloths at every seat can be seen through the windows of the 1st Class Pullman car 'Carina'. This coach, which was built in 1951, was in the train that formed the final run of the 'Golden Arrow' in 1972, ending an era of elegance in Continental travel.

MARITIME HERITAGE

officials would not agree to do likewise on the English side; such inspections had to be carried out at Dover.

In 1929, three years after the inauguration of these luxury boat-trains, the Southern Railway introduced a new steamer, *Canterbury*, specifically for the 'Golden Arrow' service. Almost 3,000 gross tons, she was built, like so many of the railway-owned steamers, by Denny Brothers of Dumbarton. Although capable of carrying over 1,500 people, she was initially restricted to just 300 1st Class passengers, who enjoyed a standard of luxury hitherto unknown on the Channel. With much use of mahogany, leather upholstery and shining brass, she brought, at long last, something of the ambience of an ocean liner to the short sea crossing. Her many amenities included a palm court tea lounge, a popular feature of the ship. The exclusiveness of this new service was emphasised on her daily departures from Dover by the sailing, 20 minutes behind her, of the ordinary Calais-bound mail-boat for those travelling 2nd Class.

Together with the Pullman trains with which she connected, *Canterbury* began a new era in cross-Channel steamer travel, one that in retrospect we would call its heyday. Everyone who was anyone travelled by this route - royalty, leading statesmen, famous film stars. Time-keeping was a matter of pride - the gleaming cream and gold coaches of the 'Golden Arrow' would pull out of Victoria Station on the dot of 11 o'clock, while their French counterparts would leave the Gare du Nord at noon. Arrival in the opposite capital would be some 6½ hours later. From 1929 a connection was also made at Calais with the new 'Côte d'Azur' Pullman train, which ran to the French Riviera.

Having embarked her passengers from the 'Golden Arrow', *Invicta*, which replaced the older *Canterbury* on the 'Golden Arrow' service in 1947, sets sail on her morning departure from Dover Harbour, bound for Calais in 1967.

With the Depression of the 1930s, however, *Canterbury* was modified to carry 2nd Class passengers in addition to the restricted number of 1sts, and 2nd Class Pullman coaches were included on the trains. Although the 'Golden Arrow' continued to enjoy a well-earned reputation for comfort and reliability, an all-1st-Class service was not to be seen on the Channel again.

In 1939 a larger replacement for the *Canterbury* was ordered, again from the Denny yard. The war intervened, however, before the new ship, *Invicta*, could be completed the following year. She was taken over by the Admiralty and after conversion as an assault landing ship saw considerable action, taking part in the Dieppe raid and in the Normandy landings. After refitting at the end of war service, she eventually made her first commercial sailing on the route for which she was intended on 15 October 1947, taking over from the *Canterbury*, which had reinstated the 'Golden Arrow' service in the spring of the previous year. *Canterbury* herself was then transferred to operate conventional sailings from Folkestone, and was finally scrapped in 1964.

Invicta, over 4,000 gross tons, was divided into elegant 1st and 2nd Class accommodation for up to 1,400 passengers, and was designed to be more spacious than her predecessor; she remained the largest passenger ship on the Channel for several years. She was a popular vessel, and continued operating almost entirely on the crossing between Dover and Calais. In comparison with the intensive operation of modern cross-Channel ferries and the need today for a fast turn-round in port, for most of her life *Invicta* undertook just one return crossing a day, spending less than 3 hours in every 24 at sea.

After the reinstatement of the 'Golden Arrow' at the end of the war, it seemed for a while that cross-Channel travel had returned to something of its former glory, although initially the constraints of post-war rationing were felt in the limited menus available in the Pullman

cars. But the 'Golden Arrow' soon became re-established as a favourite and elegant way to cross to France.

Pride in the train itself was reflected in the care lavished on the locomotive that hauled it. The steam engine would appear polished and gleaming from its depot each morning, bearing the 'Golden Arrow' headboard at the front, large arrows along each side, and the Union and tricolour flags fluttering above the buffers, as it backed up to the waiting Pullmans at Victoria. All the way down the line to Dover people would pause to watch the train thunder past. Everyone knew that the 'Golden Arrow' was special!

It wasn't long, however, before increasing competition was being felt from the airlines, and the patronage of 1st Class passengers began to decline. Apart from the dedicated few for whom an aeroplane could never replace the ambience of luxury rail and sea travel, increasing numbers opted for the speed of flying. For the majority, it seemed, it was better to arrive than to travel.

Timings, too, slipped, and a journey that had previously taken less than 7 hours now took more than 8. For a while, during the 1950s, the outward 'Golden Arrow' was routed through Folkestone, a move that was not popular with regular passengers. The outward sailing was usually taken by the French steamer *Côte d'Azur*, but inward sailings continued to be made by *Invicta* into Dover. Normal routings were re-established in 1960, and *Invicta* once again carried 'Golden Arrow' passengers in both directions.

Invicta alongside the Maritime station at Calais in 1967. Her passengers have disembarked to proceed through the customs hall, and the unloading of mailbags commences from *Invicta*'s forward hold. Meanwhile, the crew clean and prepare the ship in readiness for her return crossing to Dover during the afternoon.

In 1961 electric locomotives took over from steam, but somehow much of the glamour attached to the train seemed to be lost. Eventually, with the increasing reluctance of passengers to pay the supplementary fare, what had been an all-Pullman train was reduced to one of ordinary Southern Region stock, with just two or three Pullman cars in the middle. It was, of course, the same in France, and by 1969 all Pullman cars had been withdrawn from the 'Flèche d'Or'. As the 1960s drew to a close, the end of a splendid service that had now outlived its usefulness became inevitable, and in the autumn of 1972 the 'Golden Arrow' made its final run. *Invicta*, having served her country with distinction for 32 years, in peacetime and in war, was laid up in Newhaven, and a few weeks later was towed to Rotterdam for breaking up. Several of the Pullman cars of the 'Golden Arrow' have since been refurbished, however, and now form part of the sumptuous British portion of the Venice-Simplon Orient Express.

One drawback that the 'Golden Arrow' could not overcome, an inconvenience voiced by not a few of its earlier patrons, was that in spite of all the plush new splendour that was introduced, one still had to transfer from the train to the ship, and back again on to a second train.

Waiting at the station platform at Calais Maritime, the steam-hauled 'Flèche d'Or' prepares to depart on its non-stop run to Paris Nord.

The notion that one might actually be able to board a train in London and alight from the same train in Paris had an appeal that the railway companies certainly did not ignore. The construction of a tunnel was the obvious answer, but, as is recounted in Chapter 9, the political will to undertake such a venture was lacking. An alternative approach was a train-ferry, to convey a whole passenger train across the Channel, and a scheme to operate such a service from Dover was first proposed in 1868, and again in 1905, but these early plans were not pursued. A similar ferry service between Newhaven and Dieppe was considered in 1911, but this, too, never materialised.

The first train-ferry service to operate from Britain opened in 1918 (although it was not the first *in* Britain, as there had earlier been such links across both the Firth of Forth and the River Tay until replaced by the two famous railway bridges). This was instigated by the Government for conveying military supplies and equipment by rail to the British forces fighting in Europe. Using three specially-built ships, regular sailings were operated across the Channel from Southampton to Dieppe and from Richborough, a port at Pegwell Bay near Ramsgate in Kent, to both Calais and Dunkirk. These services continued after the First World War until 1923, when the ships and the terminal facilities at Southampton and Richborough were purchased by Great Eastern Train Ferries Ltd. This newly formed company had been established to operate a train-ferry service for freight from the East Coast port of Harwich to Zeebrugge, in co-operation with both the London & North Eastern Railway (LNER) and Belgian State Railways. The ships were transferred to this route, and the installations at the other ports dismantled.

In 1930, with the most recent plans for a Channel Tunnel being abandoned yet again, the Southern Railway, in conjunction with its French partner, the Nord, began detailed planning for a passenger train-ferry service to operate between Britain and France. The English terminal was to be at Dover, although Richborough, the site of the earlier military service, had been considered. Calais was the original choice on the French side, but this was later changed to Dunkirk, when it became apparent that arrangements there could be completed more rapidly.

Three specially constructed train-ferries were to be supplied for the route by the Southern Railway, and two special sleeping-car trains would be built by Wagon-Lits, the Belgian-based International Sleeping Car Company that had established the famed 'Orient Express' in the last century and now operated sleeping-cars, dining saloons and *trains de luxe* all over Europe.

These Continental-style trains, which had to be built to the smaller British loading gauge, would run nightly in each direction between London and Paris. They would be hauled, on each side of the Channel, by locomotives belonging to the respective railways. During the day the ferries would be used for conveying railway freight across the Channel. Ordinary deck passengers would also be carried on the train-ferry sailings, and - a great innovation - provision was made for the conveyance of up to 25 motor cars, which could be driven on board to a garage on the upper deck via a ramp alongside the ship. Thus not only was a through service of overnight passenger trains to be introduced between Britain and the Continent, but the first drive-on, drive-off cross-Channel car-ferry was being inaugurated at the same time!

Dunkirk, 40 kilometres east of Calais, had grown from an eighth-century fishing harbour to become the third port of France. Its development really began after the town was bought from the English by Louis XIV in 1662. Dunkirk possesses an extensive system of enclosed docks that are entered from the sea through locks, thus providing a constant water level independent of the tides. The construction of the train-ferry berth, requiring a railway ramp, or link-span, to connect with the stern of the ship, was therefore reasonably straightforward. A Maritime railway station had already been built in the docks in 1927 for a steamer service from Tilbury, on the River Thames; this service was operated by Angleterre-Lorraine-Alsace Société Anonyme de Navigation (ALA). The Southern Railway purchased a controlling interest in ALA and transferred its English terminal to Folkestone, pending the commencement of the new train-ferry operation from Dover when the ALA service would be closed.

At Dover, which has a tidal harbour subject to considerable variations in water level and a frequent heavy swell, the establishment of a suitable berth for the train-ferries was more difficult. Construction of a special dock was necessary in which the level of the ship could be raised by pumping in water until the ship's train deck was level with the shoreside rail tracks. The building of this dock, at the south-west corner of the harbour close to the Marine station, proved far more difficult than anticipated, due to the constant ingress of water through the chalk foundations and the pounding of violent winter seas against the dam that had been built across the dock entrance. Although the work came close to being abandoned, it was, with much ingenuity, eventually completed successfully. However, because of the difficulties experienced, the start of the service was delayed by more than a year.

Meanwhile, as construction work at the terminals was being undertaken, three train-ferry ships were being built on the Tyne by Swan Hunter & Wigham Richardson Ltd. As was the custom with the Southern Railway, the new vessels were named after places served by the company's trains, and they were launched in 1934 as *Hampton Ferry*, *Shepperton Ferry* and *Twickenham Ferry*. Because of the delays at Dover, they had to lie idle for some months at Southampton after delivery. They were nearly indentical turbine-powered ships of 2,900 gross tons, with a modest speed of 16.5 knots, and were distinctive with their two slender funnels positioned side by side. Originally coal-fired and loaded directly from coal wagons run on to the ship, they were later converted to burn oil.

Four rail tracks, which converged to two at the stern, were recessed into the train deck, and the ships could carry either 12 sleeping-cars or up to 40 specially built freight wagons. Both 1st and 2nd Class dining and general saloons were located on the upper deck for the use of passengers not using the through overnight train, and each ship had a total capacity of 500 persons. Sleeping-car passengers were free to use the facilities on board during the night crossing if they wished (narrow platforms having been installed on the train deck), but most preferred to remain in their berths. Since, however, much shunting took place at both ferry terminals, and the carriages had to be jacked up off their springs and shackled to the deck by chains while at sea, one had to be a very heavy sleeper indeed to be unaware that this was no ordinary train journey!

The sleeping-cars were handsomely furnished with every comfort. Each compartment, richly decorated in blue with silver fittings, had plenty of mirrors, electric lighting, and a compact hand-basin, with either a single or a double berth of generous size. Each car, at least initially, had its own conductor, who could be summoned at the push of a bell to supply drinks and light refreshments or, for those who couldn't forget they were at sea, something to counter *mal de mer*. Breakfast could be taken in the dining-car, which was attached to the end of the train after it had crossed the Channel, although this was not always available in France. Customs and passport formalities were taken care of at the rail termini at the beginning and end of the journey. And although there are certain things you are not allowed to do on a train while standing in a station, modern engineering ensured that on this train, on board a ship, you could!

The new through service, called the 'Night Ferry', was inaugurated between London and Paris on the night of 14 October 1936, leaving Victoria at 10 pm and the Gare du Nord at 9.50. Arrival was before 9 o'clock the following morning. It was a strange sight indeed to see the Continental blue and gold sleeping-cars sweeping through the Kent countryside, each coach bearing the legend 'Compagnie Internationale des Wagon-Lits et des Grands Express Européens', and it was a unique experience to be able to board such a train in the very heart of London. The 1st Class single fare in 1936 was £4 19s 6d.

The 'Night Ferry' soon became, along with the 'Golden Arrow', the fashionable way to cross. But it offered two things the 'Golden Arrow' never could: the convenience of not having to change en route and, for those who wished it, absolute privacy. Its most famous passenger during its earlier years was the Duke of Windsor, who travelled this way from France on his private visits to England. On one occasion after the war he was forced to change trains in the early hours of the morning when some of the coaches forming the 'Night Ferry' were derailed at Dunkirk.

Before the war only two of the train-ferries were usually in operation at any one time, the third being kept as a reserve vessel, but as rail freight and conventional passenger business developed, so more day crossings were introduced between Dover and Dunkirk. In 1937, in response to French patriotic feeling over what had been regarded as an Anglo-French operation, the *Twickenham Ferry* was transferred to the French flag under the owner-

The Brussels car of the 'Night Ferry'. Through the windows can be seen the doors of the sleeping compartments. On the side of the coach (right) is the crest of the Wagon-Lits Company, which operated the 'Night Ferry' trains until 1977. This particular sleeping car, number 3792, is now in the National Railway Museum in York, where it was photographed in 1981, and was one of the original pre-war set built in France for the 'Night Ferry'. Taken to Germany during the war, it was afterwards discovered, badly damaged, in Poland. Returned to Wagon-Lits and restored, it was finally withdrawn from 'Night Ferry' service in 1974.

ship of the ALA, but she retained her very English name; flying the tricolour and with 'Dunkerque' as the port of registry on her stern always seemed a strange contradiction!

The Second World War brought a sudden halt to the 'Night Ferry'. The sleeping-cars that had arrived at Victoria station on the morning of 4 September 1939 were shipped back to France, empty, later the same day. All three train-ferries were subsequently taken into military service.

As the war developed, a more sinister use for the Dover-Dunkirk train-ferry link was being planned. Hitler had given orders that the train-ferry installations at the two ports should not be destroyed. He had decided that Dover Castle, with its commanding position overlooking the town of Dover and the Eastern Channel, was to be his official residence in England, and that he would effect his triumphal entry into a defeated Britain by special train on board the ferry from Dunkirk. Thankfully, this was not to be, and while this is not a book about the war service of cross-Channel steamers, we should record the gallantry of their crews, who now found themselves serving on landing craft, minesweepers and assault ships, where hitherto these same vessels had been ships of pleasure, business and trade.

After the war the 'Night Ferry' service restarted, from Paris, on 14 December 1947, and in both directions the following night, and the allure and ambience of Continental rail travel returned to a rather austere post-war Britain. On the following New Year's Day nationalisation of the railways came into effect, and what had been the Southern Railway became the Southern Region of British Railways. As life returned to normal, and Britons could once more venture across to the European continent, traffic steadily built up, and the train-ferry service became very successful.

The need for a fourth ship, and the desire to participate in the train-ferry operation by the Société Nationale des Chemins de Fer Francais (SNCF - French National Railways, which had taken over control of the railways of France in 1937), led to an order being placed for a more modern vessel. The new French ship, *Saint-Germain*, entered service in 1951. She was designed and built by the Elsinore Shipping Co of Denmark, who had considerable experience in constructing train-ferries, which operate on several routes linking the Danish islands with the mainland. As a result *Saint-Germain* had a decidedly Scandinavian look. Because of concerns over the possible construction of a Channel Tunnel, she was built with extra clearance on the train deck to accommodate full-size Continental rolling-stock (which is unable to run in Britain), with the idea that should the tunnel materialise, she could be transferred to operate on a Mediterranean route.

Although she had the same general layout as the earlier ships, since she had, of course, to use the same terminal facilities, *Saint-Germain* had a sleeker profile, with a single funnel and raked masts, appearing perhaps rather ahead of her time. With accommodation for 850 passengers, her interior was gracefully furnished with much use of wood panelling, and she became a popular vessel with devotees of the Dunkirk route. Sleeping-car passengers, of course, would be unaware of the identity of the ship on which they were sailing, although the overheard and not-very-muted chatterings of the loading-gangs, as they chained the coaches to the deck, would usually give away its country of registration!

In 1956 a through service to Brussels was added to the 'Night Ferry', using one or two sleeping-cars as necessary, which connected with the Paris train at Lille. Between Brussels and Lille these coaches were attached to the end of a local train. A London-Basle sleeper was also included in 1967, but this was not a success and was discontinued early in 1969.

During the 1960s there arose the need to replace the ageing original trio of train-ferries with new tonnage, but, as before, there were concerns that a Channel Tunnel could render any new ship obsolete. It was felt that if a tunnel were built, the train-ferry service would be the first casualty. The solution to this dilemma, as the need for replacement became urgent, was to design a multi-purpose vessel; that is, a train-ferry built to fit the existing docking installations at both Dunkirk and Dover, but with the capability of operating on other routes as a conventional bow-and-stern-loading car-ferry. The first of these new ships, built by Tyne-based Swan Hunter (Shipbuilders) Ltd for Sealink, as the shipping division of British Railways was now known, was the 4,400 gross ton *Vortigern*, named after the fifth-century prince of southeast Britain. She entered service in the summer of 1969, initially as a car-ferry between Dover and Boulogne, but began operating on the 'Night Ferry' run that autumn, when *Hampton Ferry* was withdrawn from service. *Vortigern* could carry up to 1,000 passengers, but this was later increased to 1,400 when she was refitted in 1978 to operate solely as a car-ferry.

Shepperton Ferry was withdrawn in 1972 and a second multi-purpose ship, the *Chartres*, built by Dubigeon-Normandie at Nantes, was introduced by SNCF in 1974. Of 4,600 tons, and with a passenger capacity of 1,400, *Chartres* operated mainly as a vehicle-ferry from Dover and Folkestone to Calais, taking relief sailings as a train-ferry between Dover and Dunkirk during the winter.

Speed across the Channel was never important for the 'Night Ferry'. Compared with daytime London-Paris connections on other routes, the schedule was a leisurely one. Even so, the crossing time between Dover and Dunkirk on both day and night sailings was up to 4 hours, surprisingly long for a distance of only 46 miles. Little more than 2 hours after leaving Dover the ferry would arrive off Dunkirk, but the rest of the time was spent passing through one of the entrance locks to enter the port, and negotiating the various dock basins to the ferry berth. On daytime sailings this was fascinating for a ship-lover, but a rather tedious business for those travellers keen to press on with their journeys. Most, therefore, opted for other routes, and the appeal of a daytime crossing on the Dover-Dunkirk ferries, if one didn't mind the time they took, was that they were never crowded. Especially when the *Saint-Germain* was running, this was a route for cross-Channel connoisseurs!

The third of the new ships to appear had been ordered by ALA in 1969 and had been due to enter service before the *Chartres*. Her Italian shipbuilders, however, went bankrupt during her construction and the new ship, *Saint Eloi*, was not completed until 1975, after the last of the original trio, *Twickenham Ferry*, had to be withdrawn following boiler failure. *Saint Eloi* was intended to operate mainly on the train-ferry route and, unlike the earlier two multi-purpose vessels, did not have bow-loading facilities for vehicles.

In 1976 a new train-ferry terminal was opened at what is called Dunkirk West, a major harbour development being established at Gravelines, a seaside resort midway between Dunkirk and Calais, and which was for centuries the port for the ancient town of St Omer. This new dock facility was tidal, but with modern locomotives an inclined link-span between the shore and the ship was no longer the problem it was when the train-ferry service first started. With no need to pass through locks, and with

a shorter distance to Dover, the crossing was reduced to little more than 2 hours. This permitted an earlier arrival of the 'Night Ferry' in London.

The following year, British Rail took over the operation and manning of the train from Wagon-Lits, but with the sleeping-cars now repainted in SNCF livery. In 1978 new timings were introduced so that one ship, usually *Saint Eloi*, could convey the sleeping-cars in both directions.

These new changes did not survive long. In its final years the 'Night Ferry' was not well promoted and it was increasingly regarded as something of an anachronism. It was by now, for example, the only passenger train through Kent that needed a locomotive to haul it, and its running costs were therefore high. Many of the sleeping-cars were from the original pre-war set, and no new ones had been built for the train since 1952. To the chagrin of many passengers, a restaurant-car was no longer attached on either side of the Channel, and breakfast had to be postponed until arrival. But while it continued to be patronised by a dedicated band of regular travellers, the train's demise was in sight. The 'Night Ferry', so to speak, had had its day.

On the evening of 31 October 1980 it set out from Victoria, Paris Nord and Brussels for its final crossing. It was the last through passenger train to connect London with the Continent - until, that is, the commencement of services through the Channel Tunnel 14 years later, accompanied by much media hype that totally ignored the remarkable rail connection that had previously linked England with mainland Europe over a period of 44 years.

Passengers continued to use the Dover-Dunkirk route, and nightly trains ran in connection with it to the Channel ports, their passengers transferring on foot to and from the ship. But this, too, ended in 1985 when the service became freight-only. *Saint Eloi* was withdrawn and sold, becoming the conventional car-ferry *King Orry* of the Isle of Man Steam Packet Company. *Saint-Germain* remained on the route, but without carrying passengers, until being finally scrapped in 1988, one of the longest-serving of any cross-Channel ferry.

It was ironic that while it had been the cancellation of the Channel Tunnel that had originally brought the train-ferries into existence, it was the renewed threat of the tunnel that continued to blight the 'Night Ferry' over the decades of its operation, bringing a reluctance to upgrade standards or to invest in new rolling-stock. The 'Night Ferry' remained to the end, in essence, a 1930s institution caught in a time warp.

The cross-Channel train-ferry was not, however, quite dead. While the tunnel was being dug beneath the sea, a new tidal train-ferry berth was being constructed above, further along Dover's Admiralty Pier. This was used by the large French train-ferry *Nord Pas-de-Calais*, introduced in 1988 for the carriage of rail freight (including hazardous cargoes prohibited in the tunnel), but not passengers, between Dover and Dunkirk West. But this new service did not long survive the opening of the Channel Tunnel. It was closed at the end of 1995 and the ship transferred to conventional cross-Channel duties as a vehicle-ferry, bringing to an end the 77-year history of train-ferry links between Britain and the Continent.

But what had also ended, and after a much longer history, was the very notion that a sea-crossing was necessary at all for those who journeyed between London and the capitals of Continental Europe. The pattern of steamer services and connecting rail links that had become established, with the black-hulled, buff-funnelled vessels hurrying back and forth across the busy waters of the Channel, and which seemed set to continue for eternity, was to be changed forever by the impact of the aeroplane, the motor car and, finally, by the long-awaited opening of the Channel Tunnel.

Above The train-ferry *Hampton Ferry*, completed in 1934 and one of the three original ships built for the new passenger train-ferry service to the Continent, seen in her original Southern Railway colours of black hull and black-topped buff funnels, as she sets sail from Dover for Dunkirk, with Dover Castle in the background. The cut-away section of deck just aft of the lifeboats indicates the position where cars were driven on to the ship's garage via a side ramp.

Below Over 30 years old and still going strong, *Hampton Ferry* in 1966, freshly painted in the new livery of British Railways (blue hull and red funnels), which was adopted after the entire railway-owned fleet came under centralised control in 1963. She was withdrawn three years later following boiler problems, but was sold in 1970 for further service in Bermuda.

Above The stern arrangement of *Hampton Ferry*. Two tracks at the stern diverge to four on the deck of the ship. The railway loading-ramp (link-span) is lowered to fit securely into the cut-away section at the stern of the vessel, engaging on the vertical 'pin' to ensure precise alignment of the railway tracks.

Below The promenade deck, twin funnels, steam whistle and traditional wooden lifeboats of *Shepperton Ferry*, showing the windows of the 1st Class dining saloon. She was withdrawn in 1972 and sold to Spanish shipbreakers.

Above right *Twickenham Ferry* sails from Dover in 1965, in the funnel colours of the Angleterre-Lorraine-Alsace Société Anonyme de Navigation (ALA), with her passengers enjoying the sunshine and the view forward from the open upper deck, a delight that is rarely possible on modern ferries. Although originally built for the Southern Railway, *Twickenham Ferry* was transferred to the French flag under the ownership of the ALA in 1937. She became the longest surviving member of the original trio of train-ferries, remaining on the Dover-Dunkirk route until 1974, by which time she was the only pre-war passenger ship still operating across the Channel.

Right The 1951-built train-ferry *Saint-Germain* running astern into Dover in 1974. A sleek and graceful vessel, she was a firm favourite with discerning travellers. The solid upright stanchions along the side give away her Danish origins. The garage section at the after end of the promenade deck, characteristic of all the passenger train-ferries that operated on the Dover-Dunkirk route, can be clearly seen.

MARITIME HERITAGE

MARITIME HERITAGE

Above left Looking across the railway marshalling yards of the train-ferry terminal at Dover in 1978, with *Saint-Germain* in the train-ferry dock. A hovercraft is leaving from the Hoverport to the left, and is just passing the old lighthouse café at the end of the Prince of Wales Pier. The enclosed walkway across the rail tracks at the stern of the ship brings foot-passengers from Dover Marine station (out of view on the right) to the train-ferry berth.

Left A view from the train-ferry as she approaches, stern first, the original terminal at Dunkirk in 1974. On the left is the terminal building and the railway station with, raised, the side-loading link-span for cars. The ramp by which cars descended from here to ground level can be seen further to the right of this. Immediately to the left of the ship's flag is the railway link-span, which will be lowered on to the stern of the vessel.

Above The railway link-span at Dunkirk with the stern of *Saint-Germain*. The long link-span was in two sections, hinged at the midway position, with a single track at the shoreward end diverging to double tracks where it connected with the ship. As can be seen from this 1974 photograph, the uneven distribution of weight on the train-deck of the ship during loading and unloading operations could result in a significant list, and the link-span needed to twist to accommodate this.

Below The multi-purpose train- and car-ferry *Vortigern* sails from Dover. The garage on the upper deck, loaded and unloaded via the side ramp when on the Dover-Dunkirk service, could also be accessed by internal ramps when the ship operated as a conventional bow-and-stern-loading car-ferry.

Left *Vortigern* undergoing maintenance in dry-dock at Southampton, showing her twin propellers, twin rudders, and the loading arrangement at the stern. The rail tracks on the deck and the same stern-docking arrangements as on the earlier vessels can be seen. In this instance a horizontal plate, for use when the vessel is operating as a conventional car-ferry, extends over the locating pin intended for the railway link-span.

Below left The French train- and car-ferry *Chartres*. Built in 1974, she spent most of her career as a conventional car-ferry operating out of Calais, serving both Folkestone and Dover, and she was the last such vessel to use the passenger facilities at Dover's Admiralty Pier prior to their closure in 1994. In her final years her funnel carried the logo of the ALA company (see cover photograph).

Below A brochure produced for the 'Night Ferry' after British Rail took over the operation of the train from the Wagon-Lits Company in 1977. Inside it begins, 'Now there's a civilised way to Paris and Brussels. . .' In fact, this 'civilised way' had started 40 years previously with many of the sleeping-cars that were still in use. But British Rail's attempts to promote the service were not enough, and the 'Night Ferry' closed permanently just three years after this brochure was produced.

Above The ALA train-ferry *Saint Eloi* leaving Dover in 1975. Unlike *Vortigern* and *Chartres*, she was not fitted with bow doors for use on conventional car-ferry routes. Following her introduction she was the mainstay of the Dover-Dunkirk train-ferry route, along with the older *Saint-Germain*, continuing until the service was closed to passengers in 1985.

Below *Saint Eloi* heads out to sea through the western entrance of Dover Harbour on a regular crossing to Dunkirk in 1985. She was sold in that year, five years after the closure of the 'Night Ferry' and the ending of what had been an ambitious and unique scheme of nightly sleeper trains linking London with the Continent.

4. THE LAST CHANNEL PACKET

It was really during the 1950s that the great, annual exodus of British holidaymakers to Continental Europe really began in earnest, and when the cross-Channel business started on its rapid growth that still continues today. Yet these same post-war years were to see the decline and eventual demise of the traditional cross-Channel packet.

These fast, often graceful ships were liners in miniature, carrying passengers, mail and a limited amount of cargo back and forth across the Channel. The term 'packet' probably originated in Stuart times, when bundles of letters and official papers were transported across the Channel between England and France. Packet-boats were, of course, originally sailing ships, but the steam packet evolved over the period of a century from the Victorian paddle steamer to the modern screw-driven vessel. Coal-firing gave way to oil, reciprocating steam engines were replaced by more powerful steam turbines, and these in turn by less romantic diesel engines. The passenger steamer had become the motor ship. More vibration, perhaps, but considerably more efficient than their predecessors. Now even the last of these traditional vessels has gone, and every passenger ship in cross-Channel service today is a car-ferry.

The Belgian Ostend company had been the first to adopt diesel-engined ships, with the *Prince Baudouin* in 1933. The British railway-owned fleet, on the other hand, was the last to abandon steam on the Channel, retaining steam-turbine propulsion until the motor-driven car-ferries *Hengist* and *Horsa* were introduced at Folkestone in 1972.

It is, of course, not necessary to go abroad in order to cross the Channel. One part of Britain that lies on the other side is that collection of several small islands close to the French coast, the Channel Islands. A popular holiday destination and a major agricultural area, they are dependent territories of the Crown and the only part of the Duchy of Normandy to remain under British rule. But although the sea routes to these islands are, in a sense, domestic rather than international services, the crossing from England is one of the longest on the Channel. Passenger sailings operated from the Channel Islands to Weymouth and Southampton, and also in earlier years right round the coast to London. The Southampton service was latterly maintained by the pre-war, twin-funnelled steamers *Isle of Jersey*, *Isle of Guernsey* and *Isle of Sark*. But this route was terminated in the early 1960s, leaving Weymouth as the principal port of embarkation for the Islands.

Weymouth had been a popular seaside resort since the 18th century, helped by the visit of George III, who came here to bathe in 1789. Its port, too, has always been busy, with a thriving coastal trade and, in the past, regular links with the New World. By the late 1950s the ships sailing from Weymouth to the Channel Islands were among the oldest in service on the Channel. *St Julien* and *St Helier*, built for the Great Western Railway in 1925, had seen extensive service by the time they were finally withdrawn in 1960. They were joined in 1948 by *St Patrick*, a name reflecting the GWR's Irish Sea connections. Although responsibility for Weymouth-based vessels was transferred to the Southern Region of British Railways following the nationalisation of 1948, *St Patrick* remained under Western Region management for her first decade of service from the Dorset port. She was later transferred, first to Southampton and later to Dover and Folkestone, where she remained on the short-sea routes until being sold to Greek shipowners in 1971.

The long-delayed introduction of new tonnage on the Channel Islands routes began in 1960, with the arrival of the first of a pair of handsome new vessels, *Caesarea*, which was joined the following year by her sister, *Sarnia*. These ships were built by J. Samuel White & Co of Cowes, the only cross-Channel ferries, other than hovercraft, to have been built on the Isle of Wight*. With accommodation for 1,400 passengers and designed for both day and night sailings, these ships provided much-improved facilities and were successful in generating considerably increased traffic to the Channel Islands. Uniquely for traditional cross-Channel passenger steamers, they were one-class ships, all passengers having the run of the entire vessel, which gave them an additional appeal on what is largely a tourist route. *Caesarea* and *Sarnia* continued on the service from Weymouth to the Channel Island harbours of St Helier and St Peter Port until their inevitable displacement by car-ferries during the 1970s.

To connect with these sailings the Channel Island boat-train from Waterloo would slowly wind its way along the edge of Weymouth's picturesque harbour to a platform on the Quay, alongside the waiting steamer. This route was along a public highway, so pedestrians and road vehicles would be held back to allow the train to pass, but progress would sometimes be delayed while a carelessly parked car was removed from the train's path.

Sarnia continued to operate seasonal sailings to the

---

* See *Maritime Heritage: White's of Cowes* by David L. Williams in this series.

Above The Channel Islands boat-train from Weymouth to Waterloo makes slow progress at the start of its journey, as it winds its way past parked cars and pedestrians along Weymouth Quay in 1983.

Like so much else that was once a familiar part of cross-Channel travel, the Weymouth boat-train is no more, and the port, too, has lost its regular and traditional link with the Channel Islands.

Right The first Southern Railway vessel to be introduced after the war was the turbine-steamer *Falaise*, named after a small inland town in Normandy. Intended primarily for the Southampton to St Malo route, she entered service in 1947 and is seen here in a painting reproduced on one of the final travel posters for the Southern Railway before it became the Southern Region of British Railways following the 1948 nationalisation. Her passenger capacity was over 1,500 in two classes, of whom approximately one-third could be accommodated in overnight cabins. In 1964 *Falaise* was withdrawn from service at Southampton and converted into a one-class stern-loading car-ferry, reducing both her gross tonnage and her passenger capacity. She inaugurated the new vehicle service between Newhaven and Dieppe, but was soon displaced by the introduction of new tonnage and was transferred to Weymouth. After several years on the Channel Islands run she was scrapped in 1974.

THE NEW T.S. "FALAISE"
SOUTHAMPTON, St. MALO AND CHANNEL ISLANDS SERVICES
SOUTHERN RAILWAY

Channel Islands until 1977, while *Caesarea* was transferred to the Kent Channel ports to operate services to Calais and Boulogne. Her final commercial sailing, and the last Channel crossing to be made by a traditional British passenger ferry, was from Boulogne to Folkestone on 4 October 1980. Dressed overall, and with a crowd of enthusiasts ashore and afloat, she closed in style a magnificent chapter in British maritime history.

Southampton's traditional cross-Channel links, not only with the Channel Islands, but also with France, were closed down in the 1960s, as will be related in Chapter 5. These routes, serving Le Havre and St Malo, had been re-opened after the war by the 1933-built Southern Railway vessel *Brittany*, later replaced by *Falaise* and *Normannia*.

At Newhaven, where sailings to Dieppe were operated jointly by the railways of Britain and France, several new mail-steamers were introduced to re-establish services after the war. The first of these was the French vessel *Londres*, actually built during the war and taken over by Germany for use as a minelayer before commencing on the route for which she had been intended in 1947. She was joined the same year by her newly built sister, *Arromanches*, and in 1952 by the more modern, sleek-looking *Lisieux*.

A new British ship, the *Brighton*, solid and powerful in appearance in contrast to the finesse of the French vessels, was introduced on the Newhaven-Dieppe service in 1951. To maintain an Anglo-French balance on the route as pre-war vessels were withdrawn, British Railways took over the running of *Londres* in 1955, although her French name was retained. The popularity of the route began to decline, however, particularly during winter periods, and a four-ship fleet became unsustainable. Gradually the vessels were laid up, and it was only with the conversion of the service to car-ferry operation that fortunes revived. All three of the French-built ships, like so many other vessels that had served on the Channel, were eventually sold to Greece. One wonders how many British tourists cruising between the Greek Islands realise that they might be sailing on an old cross-Channel ferry! For those in the know, catching sight of a forgotten favourite in a new guise in Piraeus Harbour, a veritable floating maritime museum, is like meeting an old friend.

In fact, *Brighton* found service elsewhere on the Channel. In 1967 she was purchased by Jersey Lines Ltd, a privately owned concern. Renamed *La Duchesse de Bretagne*, she began operating to the Channel Islands and St Malo from both Torquay and Weymouth, and with a top speed of 24 knots was claimed to be the fastest ship in Channel service. Her interior accommodation had been refurbished, and among new features introduced on board was an attractive English-style pub. *La Duchesse* had also been modified to carry up to 20 cars, which could be driven from the quayside on to the after deck by means of ramps on either side of the ship. She thus introduced the first car-ferry service to the Channel Islands.

The following year she switched her UK ports to Plymouth and Southampton, with a very complex weekly schedule. Not helped, presumably, by confusion over which port she was sailing from and when, heavy losses ensued and in 1969 her owners went bankrupt. The ship herself was arrested in Southampton for unpaid debts, to be sold eventually to Belgian shipbreakers, an ignominious end to a fine ship, one of the last traditional steamers to have been built by the famous yard of Denny Brothers.

For many years until the 1970s on the short-sea routes from Dover and Folkestone, British ships tended to operate to Boulogne while French ships served Calais (the main exception being *Canterbury*, then *Invicta*, on the 'Golden Arrow' route). In 1925 the Southern Railway introduced two new steamers, *Isle of Thanet* and *Maid of Kent*, for service across the Dover Strait, and these were joined five years later by two new French ships, *Côte d'Azur* and *Côte d'Argent*. Three of these vessels were lost during the war, and only *Isle of Thanet* survived, to continue in service until 1963.

The need for heavier and longer boat-trains had led to an upgrading of the railway lines through Kent, and by 1925 a total of 25 bridges on the Victoria-Tonbridge-Dover line had been rebuilt. The typical pattern of services consisted of three boat-trains a day from Victoria to connect with sailings from Dover to Calais, three in each direction for the Dover-Ostend route, and two for Folkestone-Boulogne. Additional relief services were operated during busy periods.

Boulogne is an important commercial centre and has become the biggest fishing port in France. It is also a popular shopping and day-trip venue with British visitors. The town, climbing up the hill from the quayside and dominated by the domed cathedral of Notre Dame within the ramparts and cobbled streets of the Ville Haute, is conveniently close to the harbour.

Calais is the quintessential Continental ferry-port, and now by far the busiest. With its modern motorway connections, cross-Channel travellers can speed on their way without any need to pass through the town. Nevertheless, though often busy with British day-trippers visiting the hypermarkets, the town does have its charms. Its most characteristic feature, readily visible from the sea (and also, on occasions, from the cliff-top at Dover), is the clock-tower of the Hotel de Ville, the Flemish-Renaissance town hall. Outside this building stands Rodin's famous statue of the Burghers of Calais, which commemorates the occasion on which these selfless public officials pleaded with Edward III when their town was under siege to take their own lives and spare the remainder of the townspeople.

From the harbour stations of both Boulogne and Calais ran direct trains across France southwards into Switzerland and Italy. However, these stations closed in 1995, thus ending the long-established system of through rail and sea connections for travellers from Britain. It was always fascinating, as one's ship pulled alongside the quay, to see these trains, made up of carriages from the French (SNCF), Swiss (SBB) and Italian (FS) railways, together with the dark blue restaurant cars and sleepers of Wagon-Lits, waiting at the station platforms. Within barely 20 miles of Kent, here was a whiff of the Alps, the Mediterranean, and the Adriatic!

For some onward-bound passengers there would be a tiring journey ahead as they sat up through the long hours of the ensuing night. Others had booked *couchettes*, six-seater compartments that could be made up into berths, three-high on each side. A few would enjoy the comfort and privacy of a proper sleeping compartment in a Wagon-Lits, or more recently in one of the TEN (Trans Euro Nacht) sleepers of the European railways' pool. Within a few hours these trains would have left far behind the salt-laden air of the Channel coast and be speeding towards the majestic scenery of the Alps. Their passengers would waken to the sight of colourful chalets, verdant grassland, rushing streams and snow-capped peaks. For many, the journey would end here, perhaps at Interlaken, always a favourite resort with British visitors to Switzerland and close to the ski-slopes of the Bernese Oberland. For services continuing into Italy and routed via Basle, breakfast could be taken in the dining-car as the train climbed up from Lake Lucerne through the amazing system of loops and spirals carved into the mountainside that lead towards the entrance of the St Gothard Tunnel. Others, travelling via Lausanne, would find themselves passing serenely through the beautiful Rhone Valley towards Brig, to continue onwards through the Simplon Tunnel.

Once through the mountains, the train would glide down past the shimmering Italian Lakes and across the Lombardy plain, to come finally to rest beneath the great arched roof of Milan's Central station, which was finally completed in 1932 after more than 20 years of construction. Observant passengers alighting here might notice, as they walked along the platform, that the formation of their train had changed since its departure from the Channel port the previous evening. Several of its carriages would have been taken off during the journey, to join other trains bound elsewhere, while new ones, perhaps from starting points in Germany or Holland, or merely on domestic services within Italy, had been attached. For trains proceeding further south towards Rome, or eastwards towards Venice and the Balkans, this process could mean that on certain services, those that were in a sense mere timetable entities rather than physical realities, no single coach actually made the entire journey from the Channel, and onward passengers would need to change carriages en route, often doing so here at Milan.

Meanwhile, much further north, the now forgotten ship that had carried these railway travellers across the Channel the previous day would have been busy ferrying other passengers to join yet other trains, providing a vital link in a truly integrated, international transport system.

Rather surprisingly, only one conventional British mail-ship, *Maid of Orleans*, has been built for the short-sea routes across the Strait of Dover since the last war. Completed in 1949, she was the last of the traditional Denny-built steam packets to remain in service. She had what was claimed at the time to be a 'commodious and luxurious' interior, attractively finished with wood veneer, and had accommodation for 886 1st and 736 2nd Class passengers. *Maid of Orleans* was the first vessel on the Dover Strait to be fitted with stabilisers, but her original short funnel caused smoke problems on the after deck, so was subsequently heightened and fitted with a distinctive 'fireman's helmet' arrangement to deflect the engine exhaust fumes clear of the stern. She operated mainly between Folkestone and Boulogne, but was later transferred to Dover. Altogether *Maid of Orleans* served successfully for 26 years until being withdrawn in 1975.

The end of the line, but not quite the end of the journey. An SNCF couchette car of the 'Italia Express', which provided a connection between Rome and London, a 24-hour journey of almost 1,200 miles and which ran via Milan, Basle, Strasburg and Lille, has arrived at Calais Maritime station in 1975 almost within sight of England. But here its passengers must transfer to the steamer for Dover and thence continue onward by a British Rail boat-train service to Victoria in order to complete the final part of their journey.

Her French consort at Folkestone was *Côte d'Azur*, built for SNCF in 1950 for its service from Calais. Rather larger than *Maid of Orleans* but with a slightly smaller passenger capacity, she served continuously on the Calais-Folkestone route until being displaced in 1972 by the French car-ferry *Chartres*.

Both *Maid of Orleans* and *Côte d'Azur* were able to carry several cars. These were lifted on and off by crane, and the two ships continued to handle vehicles in this manner, as did other mail-ships, for some time after drive-on, drive-off car-ferry services began to operate from Dover.

The largest fleet of cross-Channel mail-ships was that of the state-owned Belgian Marine Administration (Regie voor Maritiem Transport - RMT). Always smart, these ships maintained a regular service between Dover and the Belgian seaside city of Ostend, which had grown during the latter part of the 19th century to become one of the most fashionable resorts in Europe. Established as a fish-

ing village on the featureless, sandy dunes of Flanders, its links with England did much to stimulate its growth as an important cosmopolitan town, and as the only harbour of any significance along this stretch of coast until the construction of Zeebrugge further east.

A new, imposing railway station and ferry terminal was opened at Ostend in 1939. From here, important onward rail connections ran to Holland, Germany, Austria and Eastern Europe. Unlike most Channel ports, the ferry quay at Ostend is close to the town's centre, and the railway station serves the need of both town and harbour. Famous named trains that regularly ran from here and connected with sailings from Dover included the Oostende-Suisse Express to Basle, Lucerne and Chur, the Oostende-Wien Express to Brussels, Cologne, Bonn, Frankfurt and Vienna, the Tauern Express, which ran via Stuttgart and Munich on to Salzburg and Zagreb, and the Nord Express to Berlin and St Petersburg (Leningrad).

Several ships of the Dover-Ostend fleet survived the Second World War, but the company soon set about introducing new vessels, all diesel-engined, to augment and update its services to England. Indeed, work was actually started, in secrecy, during the German occupation. Sister-ships *Koning Albert* and *Prince Philippe* joined the route in 1949. These were fast motor ships, with a passenger capacity of over 1,500. In addition, for night sailings, they had 21 double-berth cabins and four general sleeping saloons. Like the railways with which they connected, these ships carried their passengers in two classes, with those in 2nd Class being relegated to the aft and lower sections of the ship, and each class had its own separate restaurants, lounges and outside deck areas. This was the arrangement that was to continue, on most cross-Channel routes, until the introduction of one-class car-ferries.

Three further passenger vessels were ordered for the Ostend-Dover service in 1954. More modern and streamlined in appearance, and introducing the distinctive 'Belgian' funnel with large vents fore and aft, they were nevertheless based very much on the earlier designs, maintaining a continuity in style that was a feature of the Ostend boats. These sister-ships, *Roi Leopold III*, *Koningin Elisabeth* and *Reine Astrid*, entered service between 1956 and 1958, providing a much-increased capacity on the fast-developing Ostend route in time for the Brussels World Fair in 1958 (for which the modern symbol of Brussels, the Atomium, had been constructed). Although car-ferry operation had already begun between Dover and Ostend by the time they entered service, these ships, too, had been designed to carry a number of cars in the hold space.

The nomenclature of these Belgian ships followed the tradition of the line in naming most of its vessels after members of the Belgian Royal Family. Since, however, Belgium has two official languages, this was done alternately in Flemish and in French.

The last and the largest conventional mail-ship to be built for the Dover-Ostend service - indeed, for any cross-Channel route, and probably the last ship of her type to be built anywhere in the world - was the exceedingly graceful *Prinses Paola*. Her yacht-like appearance was a familiar sight in the Channel from 1966, when she was built, until 1987 when she was finally withdrawn - truly the end of an era. Of nearly 4,500 tons, she carried up to 1,700 people, as had the earlier trio, but spread over more decks. Her 600 1st Class passengers, in particular, enjoyed finely appointed public rooms, especially the verandah bar facing forward. The Channel car-ferry was already well-established by the time *Prinses Paola* was built, but her career of over 20 years underlines just how long that transition actually took. But she was to be the last of the miniature liners, the final Channel packet.

If the post-war cross-Channel mail-ship represented the evolution of more than a century of maritime development, then the elegant *Prinses Paola* was the summit of that achievement. How fitting, then, that she should be a Belgian ship, the last traditional vessel of a shipping line that had for long been pace-setters on the Channel.

Above St Patrick was built for the Great Western Railway, which was nationalised and absorbed into British Railways three weeks before she was delivered in 1948. Intended for services to Ireland from Holyhead and to the Channel Islands from Weymouth, she subsequently operated on most of the railway-owned routes across the English Channel, retaining throughout her original name from Great Western days. She is seen here sailing out of Boulogne bound for Folkestone, a route on which she served for several years during the late 1960s. She was finally withdrawn in 1971.

Below Breaking a long tradition of class-segregated travel ashore and afloat, *Caesarea*, the first of a pair of one-class passenger ships for the Channel Islands service, was introduced at Weymouth in 1960. She is seen here on a summer sailing from the Dorset port in 1967.

Left *La Duchesse de Bretagne* was converted to carry 20 cars on two decks at the stern. Loading was by means of ramps at the side of the ship. She sailed to the Channel Islands and France from various South Coast ports, but after only two seasons her owners went bankrupt and the ship was seized in Southampton for unpaid debts, eventually being sold for breaking up.

Above A traditional view at Folkestone in 1968 as passengers, having arrived at Folkestone Harbour station on the boat-train from London, crowd up the gangway on to the open deck of the 1950-built French steamer *Côte d'Azur*. Behind them come porters pushing luggage trolleys.

Right *Côte d'Azur*, named after an earlier vessel that was sunk in the last war, sets sail from Folkestone for Calais, a route on which she served throughout her 22-year career on the Channel. She was afterwards sold and sailed to the Mediterranean, but was not a success for her new owners and was scrapped two years later.

CROSSING THE CHANNEL

Maid of Orleans was completed in 1949, and was the only traditional mail-ship built for British Railways after the war for service across the Dover Strait. Smoke problems on the after deck resulted in the 'fireman's helmet' attachment being fitted to her funnel. She is seen here in 1967.

Maid of Orleans transferred from Folkestone to Dover in 1973 to provide a connection for rail passengers between London and Paris, following the closure of the 'Golden Arrow' Pullman service and the withdrawal of *Invicta*. She is seen here backing towards her berth in Dover Harbour. *Maid of Orleans* was withdrawn in 1975 and sold to Spanish shipbreakers.

In 1977 the Channel-Island steamer *Caesarea* transferred from Weymouth to operate across the Dover Strait as a replacement for *Maid of Orleans*, and is seen here preparing to sail from the Gare Maritime at Boulogne. She was the last conventional British mail-ship to operate on the Channel and made her final crossing in October 1980. She was then sold to new owners in Hong Kong. The other ships in this photograph are (left) the French car-ferry *Compiegne* and (right) Normandy Ferries' *Lion*.

MARITIME HERITAGE

Above Launched during the centenary year of the Dover-Ostend service in 1946, *Koning Albert* was completed in 1948 and is seen here 20 years later at the ferry quay at Ostend alongside the railway station. Ahead of her lies the newer mail-ship *Roi Leopold III*. Leaders in marine technology and running at one time the largest passenger fleet on the Channel, the Belgian Marine Administration (RMT) adopted diesel engines for all vessels built after 1934. Other cross-Channel operators stayed with steam propulsion for many more years.

Below *Prince Philippe*, a sister-ship to *Koning Albert*, entered service in 1949, and is here seen here in 1966 leaving Dover Harbour. A unique feature of these Belgian vessels was the arrangement of three enclosed bridge-houses.

Left With passenger numbers growing, three more mail-ships were ordered by the Belgian company for the Dover-Ostend route in 1954. The first of these, which was completed in 1956, was *Roi Leopold III*, sailing here from Ostend in 1968. All three of these ships were of similar design and were in essence updated versions of the earlier pair.

Right *Koningin Elisabeth*, which entered service in 1957, pulls away from Dover's Admiralty Pier at the start of her 3½-hour crossing to Ostend.

Koningin Elisabeth arrives stern-first at Dover, with crowds thronging her lower, 2nd Class, deck. Those on the upper deck travelling 1st Class enjoy more spacious accommodation. Given the crowded conditions often experienced on Channel crossings during peak periods, 2nd Class rail travellers would frequently upgrade to 1st for the sea portion of a through journey.

MARITIME HERITAGE

Above The third ship of the 1950s trio of Belgian passenger ferries was *Reine Astrid*, seen here pounding across the Channel in 1973 at over 23 knots. The Belgian ships joined the Sealink consortium in 1971, but although having 'Sealink' painted along their sides, they adopted their own distinctive RMT logo for the funnel.

Below With perhaps the most graceful lines of any cross-Channel ferry, the sleek and handsome *Prinses Paola* entered service between Ostend and Dover in 1966. She was the last conventional passenger ship to operate across the Channel, and was not finally withdrawn from service until 1987.

5. THE CHANNEL MOTORWAY

Soon after motor cars began appearing on public roads, the first vehicles were being shipped across the Channel by enthusiastic owners, keen to exploit the new freedom that a motoring holiday could provide. At first cars were simply crated, treated as ordinary freight, and sent by cargo steamer, the hapless driver often arriving on the Continent in the mail-ship long before his vehicle caught up with him. Later, cars began to be carried as cargo on the passenger ships, and the vehicle's owner would have the unnerving experience of watching his precious motor car being unceremoniously swung out from the quayside, hanging precariously beneath a harbour crane. All petrol had to be drained from the tank, for which no compensation was given, and damage to vehicles through knocks and scratches was not uncommon. It was a frustrating and, indeed, expensive business. The loading gangs expected heavy tips, while for the shipping companies cars were a nuisance, occupying deck space that could otherwise be used by passengers. High charges were therefore levied, on the basis that anyone who ran a motor car could afford it.

One man who thought there ought to be a better way was Captain Stuart Townsend. His family had been in shipping since the 1880s, and his father and uncle established the firm of Townsend Brothers in 1889. Originally they operated sailing ships across the Atlantic and to the Middle East, but in the early years of this century they concentrated mainly on ship management, cargo forwarding and ship delivery (this last activity being a profitable business in the days when Britain was shipbuilder to the world).

Stuart Townsend was a keen motorist, and began driving abroad in 1906, at the age of 18. That year he travelled through Spain with his mother, and their vehicle caused quite a stir everywhere they stopped. On this occasion the car had been shipped direct to Malaga by cargo vessel, while they themselves crossed the Continent by train. On subsequent trips Townsend took his car across on the Channel mail-boats, where it would often be the only vehicle on board. After one such crossing Townsend was annoyed to find that it had been damaged. On another occasion, when homeward-bound through France, Townsend misjudged the tricky requirement of having to arrive at the Channel port with the minimum amount of fuel in the tank, and had to acquire the services of a local horse for the final stretch of the journey, to tow him on to the quayside at Boulogne!

With the aim of improving services for cross-Channel motorists and decreasing the charges that they had to pay, Townsend commissioned a study in 1927 to examine the feasibility of running a dedicated car-carrying vessel across to France. This study confirmed that such a service should be profitable, given the increasing numbers of people wishing to take their cars abroad, and showed furthermore that fares could be set at half those being charged by the Southern Railway.

He therefore chartered a small 400-ton coaster, the *Artificer*, and began his new service between Dover and Calais in July 1928. This vessel, which berthed at the Camber alongside the Eastern Arm of Dover Harbour, had a capacity for 15 cars but could only carry 12 passengers, so most passengers were taken by coach to board the Southern Railway's conventional mail-steamer at the other side of the harbour. On arrival at Calais, they were again taken by coach from the passenger terminal at the Gare Maritime, around to the Quai Paul Devot where the *Artificer* would berth. Since those passengers who did travel on the *Artificer* were separated from the area where the vehicles were stowed, the Board of Trade permitted petrol to remain in the vehicles' tanks.

Loading and unloading was still carried out by crane, but at a single fare of only £2 for cars (the Southern Railway charged £3 15s 0d), here at last was a service that catered specifically for the motorist, rather than conveying his vehicle under sufferance. Although at the start the AA and RAC were slow to give this new venture their support, enthusiastic publicity was given by both *The Autocar* magazine and by the Civil Service Motoring Association. From its first year the service was a success, and the following March the company of Townsend Brothers Car Ferries was formally established.

Recognising that this was a growing business that ought not to be neglected, the Southern Railway decided to run a similar vessel of its own, and purchased a cargo steamer that was being built on the Clyde and had her modified to carry cars. She was named *Autocarrier*, and on her introduction into service in 1929 the SR reduced its fares for the conveyance of automobiles to the level charged by Townsend. The car-ferry battle had begun!

The following year Townsend Brothers acquired an ex-naval minesweeper, which was being sent to the breaker's yard. This ship, *Ford* (renamed *Forde* because of another merchant vessel of the same name), was converted to carry 30 vehicles and 168 passengers, who no longer needed to be conveyed on separate ships.

Forde was also equipped with a stern loading gate, because Stuart Townsend had another forward-looking dream: to dispense with crane-loading and allow vehicles to be driven directly on and off the ship, regardless of the state of the tide. To make use of this, however, he had to wait until the port authorities could be persuaded to install the necessary dock facilities. This was not to happen until after the Second World War, and even then the first vehicle ramp or link-span to be constructed at Calais was provided at the Townsend company's own expense.

As we have seen, a small number of cars had begun to be carried on the newly introduced train-ferry route between Dover and Dunkirk in 1936. In the same year a car-carrying service also commenced on the Dover to Ostend route, using the converted mail-ship *Ville de Liège* of 1913. She was given the new name *London-Istanbul*, to mark a planned new highway that was to pass through Belgium, Germany, Austria, Hungary, Yugoslavia and Bulgaria to Turkey, and so link Ostend with Istanbul. Even today very few British motorists venture that far! *London-Istanbul* carried 250 passengers and 100 cars, which at Ostend were driven on and off the ship through a side ramp.

After war service with the Royal Navy, Townsend's *Forde* restarted on the Dover-Calais crossing in 1947. The same year the Southern Railway introduced a larger car-carrier to operate between Dover and Boulogne. She was the *Dinard*, 1,800 gross tons and converted from a passenger vessel originally built in 1926 for service between Southampton and St Malo; she had capacity for 70 cars and 400 passengers. Townsend, too, soon needed a larger ship to cater for the growing motor car trade and also to be able to compete successfully with its rivals. Two years later the company acquired from the Admiralty the 1944-built 'River' Class frigate *Halladale* and had her converted into a stern-loading car-ferry to replace the *Forde*.

Credit for the first purpose-built, stern-loading cross-Channel car-ferry (as opposed to conversions of older vessels) belongs to the Belgian Marine Administration, RMT. This company introduced its new 2,600-ton *Car Ferry* in June 1949, to run between Ostend and Dover. She was built by the Belgian yard of Cockerill's, constructors of many of the Ostend-Dover vessels. With her squat funnel, three bridge houses and upright masts, her appearance was similar to that of the earlier Belgian mail-ships. *Car Ferry* carried 100 cars and had accommodation for 700 passengers in one class, confirming the arrangement that continued until the last passenger-only mail-ship left the Channel in the 1980s, whereby the mail-ships carried on the tradition of two-class passenger accommodation while all car-ferries had only one. For many years when the two types of vessel ran in parallel, foot passengers (as ordinary passengers not travelling in accompanied vehicles have become rather disparagingly known) were not encouraged to travel on the car-ferries from Dover. Interestingly enough, now that one-class operation has become the norm, some operators have introduced segregated lounges reserved either for the sole use of motorists and their passengers, or for any passengers opting to pay a supplementary fee.

A general view of Ostend harbour in 1968, looking across the marina towards the original car-ferry berth.

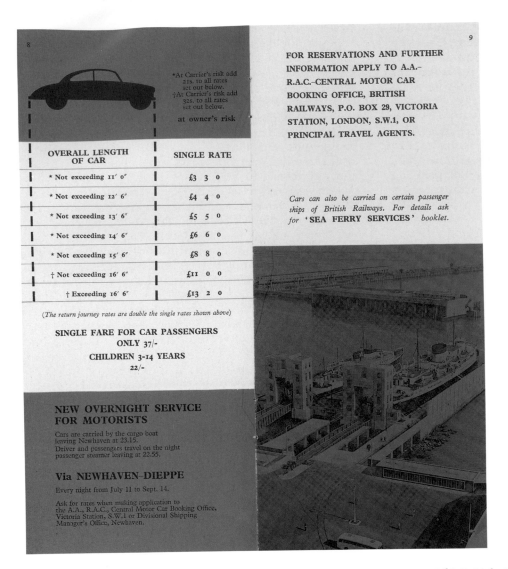

Part of a 1958 brochure advertising the sailings of *Dinard*, *Lord Warden* and the brand new *Compiegne*. In that year these ships represented the entire cross-Channel car-ferry fleet of British and French Railways (with the exception of the Dover-Dunkirk train-ferries). Up to five daily crossings were offered at peak periods to Boulogne and two to Calais, and car-sleeper trains to connect with certain sailings ran to Dover from both Manchester and Newcastle. Off-season sailings were, however, limited to one return crossing a day to both Boulogne and Calais. Less than one page of the brochure described the ships and five pages covered sailings and fares, but there were eight pages dedicated to giving practical advice on motoring abroad, reflecting the novelty of such an experience for many people.

company brought not only cash, but also business expertise to add to the Townsend company's skills in running ships. The ferry line was re-styled simply Townsend Ferries but, still operating the elderly *Halladale*, it now desperately needed a modern, larger replacement.

It still seemed for a while that the business started 40 years previously by Stuart Townsend, the originator of the cross-Channel car-ferry, might not survive. *Halladale* did, however, continue in service for another three years, until eventually replaced in 1962 by the *Free Enterprise*, a fine new 2,600 ton ship of unique design, built at Schiedam in Holland, the yard that supplied many of the company's subsequent vessels. She was the first of a veritable dynasty of increasingly sophisticated cross-Channel car-ferries. Later renamed *Free Enterprise I*, she brought Townsend Ferries back to the forefront of cross-Channel operations, a position it has retained, through amalgamations, takeovers and name changes, right up to the present day as P&O European Ferries. *Free Enterprise* also introduced a new colour-scheme to the Dover Strait. In place of the long-traditional black hull, she sported one of bright green, chosen, it is said, by George Nott himself on catching sight of Cunard's green-hulled cruise ship *Caronia* (the 'Green Goddess') sailing through the Channel!

In 1965 British Railways introduced its latest car-ferry, *Dover*, which brought new standards of decor and comfort to railway-owned ships, although much of it of the brightly coloured plastic variety, a 1960s fashion that soon went out of vogue. Built on the Tyne by Swan Hunter, her name was the result of a nationwide competition, won by a Dover man! Still turbine-powered, traditionally minded British Railways was the last operator on the Channel to change from steam-ships to motor-driven propulsion. *Dover* later moved to service across the Irish Sea, beginning a trend of much-increased interchangeability of ferries between routes. She returned, however, after conversion for drive-through operation, and with the adoption by British Railways of a new shipping nomenclature based on local historical personages, she was renamed *Earl Siward*.

Dover's car-ferry terminal was enlarged during the mid-1960s to cater for the considerable increase in ferry traffic, and a large area of the harbour was reclaimed seawards of the original customs hall and terminal building. It has continued to be extended, with the addition of new ferry berths, at frequent intervals since.

As car travel to the Continent increased, car-carrying sleeper trains were introduced from both Calais and Boulogne for onward journeys to the South of France,

Austria, Italy and Spain. These became popular with British motorists who wished to avoid the lengthy drive south, and remain so today (running from the motorail terminal at Calais), whether one crosses by ferry or by tunnel.

Further west, as the 1960s dawned, British Railways was still operating conventional mail-ships on its longer overnight services from Southampton to Le Havre and St Malo, using the Denny-built vessels *Falaise*, built in 1947, and *Normannia*, of 1952. Passenger levels had, however, been declining for some time, and the Southampton service was now proving uneconomic to operate. Considerable investment in new tonnage would be needed to upgrade the route and to develop it as a modern car-ferry operation. Instead, British Railways decided to concentrate on the shorter crossings to France, in particular by introducing a car-ferry service between Newhaven and Dieppe in conjunction with its French operating partners. BR therefore announced its intention to cease completely all passenger operations from Southampton after 1963. Both *Falaise* and *Normannia* were withdrawn and converted into stern-loading car-ferries, primarily by using lower-deck space previously occupied by passenger cabins. In 1964 *Falaise* inaugurated the new vehicle service from Newhaven, while *Normannia* transferred to assist on the Dover-Boulogne route.

For car owners the traditional railway port of Newhaven was more accessible from many parts of the country than was Dover, and the route also landed them further south than Calais or Boulogne. The introduction of a car-ferry service on the 4-hour crossing to Dieppe therefore proved popular. Dieppe itself, a Norman port, had become fashionable as a pre-war seaside resort, and was still popular amongst the French for *le weekend*. The ferries from Newhaven arrived right in the centre of the town at the Quai Henri IV, close to the shops, bistros and restaurants.

A new terminal building was constructed at Newhaven and two brand new sister ships were built for the route at St Nazaire. The twins, *Villandry* and *Valencay*, French flagged and crewed but jointly owned between France and Britain in the peculiar ratio 37:19 (see Chapter 2), entered service in 1965, joining the converted *Falaise*. They displaced the older mail-ships that had been operating on this route, and therefore carried, in addition to those with cars, rail-connected passengers travelling between London and Paris. The new ships were innovative motor vessels, although their external appearance was somewhat marred by a rather squat, diminutive funnel. They were, however, an immediate success, and traffic levels increased rapidly on what had previously been a declining route. Like several other car-ferries, both *Villandry* and *Valencay* were enlarged later in their careers by the construction of an extra vehicle deck in order to increase capacity as traffic levels continued to grow.

The first purpose-built cross-Channel car-ferry, *Prinses Josephine Charlotte*, berthed at Ostend in 1968. She was completed in 1949 and originally given the uninspiring name of *Car Ferry*, but this was changed in 1952. Her design was based heavily on that of the two Belgian mail-ships, *Koning Albert* and *Prince Philippe*, which were built at about the same time. Cars were loaded on and off the ship via a ramp at Ostend, but still had to be crane-lifted at Dover until the car-ferry terminal opened there in 1953.

Left Brought into service in time for the Brussels World Fair in 1958, *Artevelde*, seen here at Dover's car-ferry terminal in 1975, could carry cars on two decks.

Below left Introduced in 1962 and slightly larger than *Artevelde* but otherwise of similar design, *Koningin Fabiola* passes the Sailors' Memorial as she heads out to sea between the breakwaters at the entrance to Ostend Harbour in 1968.

Above With a sleeker profile than earlier Dover-Ostend vessels, the RMT car-ferry *Roi Baudouin* is seen berthed at Ostend. Built in 1965, she was enlarged to increase her capacity in 1973.

Right The British Railways car-ferry *Lord Warden* sails out of Boulogne with a happy crowd of waving holidaymakers bound for Dover. Built in 1952, she was a near-sister to the Irish Sea ferry *Princess Victoria*, which sank in heavy seas in 1953 with the loss of 133 lives when water flooded the car deck. As a result of this accident, modifications were carried out to *Lord Warden*. After lengthy service for British Railways, *Lord Warden* was sold in 1980 to Saudi Arabia and renamed *Al Zaher*.

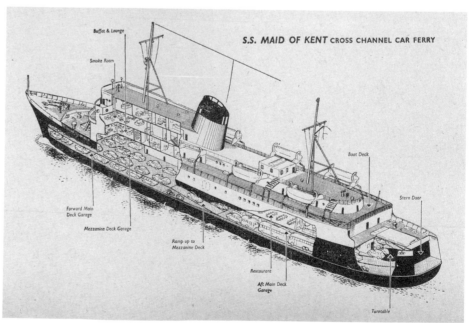

S.S. MAID OF KENT CROSS CHANNEL CAR FERRY

Buffet & Lounge

Smoke Room

Boat Deck

Forward Main Deck Garage

Mezzanine Deck Garage

Ramp up to Mezzanine Deck

Stern Door

Restaurant

Aft Main Deck Garage

Turntable

Above left The French Railways *Compiegne*, introduced in 1958, arrives at Calais from Dover in 1966, and heads astern towards the quay. The first French cross-Channel car-ferry, she also provided the first direct competition to Townsend Brothers on the Dover-Calais route. As she sails into the harbour, members of her crew, dressed in the traditional sailors' uniform that is seldom seen today on merchant ships, prepare for arrival at the ferry berth.

Left After arrival, cars unload through *Compiegne*'s stern-door at the port's original car-ferry berth.

Above The handsome vessel *Maid of Kent*, which operated between Dover and Boulogne for many years following her completion in 1959. She was subsequently transferred to Weymouth to inaugurate a new car-ferry service from there to Cherbourg.

Above right Anatomy of a 1950s car-ferry. *Maid of Kent* had internal arrangements that were typical of the cross-Channel car-ferries of the period. The loading and unloading of vehicles took place through the stern door, and although there was sufficient clearance on the after end of the car deck for the carriage of coaches and caravans, the forward section accommodated only private cars, on both the main and mezzanine decks. There was a turntable forward to assist in the manoeuvring of vehicles, which had, of course, to reverse before unloading. There was no capability for conveying commercial freight vehicles, which were not permitted on passenger ferries at Dover until 1966. *Maid of Kent* had the usual catering outlets, but the on-board fare available was basic by modern standards and there were certainly no pretensions to style with regard to the naming and decor of the facilities. With simply a restaurant, a buffet lounge and a smoke room bar (and no extensive duty-free supermarket), it was very much British Railways at sea. In spite of this, *Maid of Kent* was widely acclaimed when new and was distinctly more ship-like that some of her successors.

Left Normannia was built in 1952 as a conventional passenger steamer for the overnight service between Southampton and Le Havre. When this service ended in 1963 she was converted to carry vehicles as a stern-loading car-ferry by utilising space previously occupied by passenger cabins, and began to operate on the Dover-Boulogne service the following year. In 1976, the year after this photograph was taken at Weymouth, she opened a new car-ferry route between Dover and Dunkirk West, which operated in parallel with the train-ferry service between the same two ports.

Right French-flagged but jointly owned by the railways of Britain and France, *Villandry* entered service with her sister *Valencay* on the newly established car-ferry crossing between Newhaven and Dieppe in 1965. She is seen here in 1967 at the car-ferry berth alongside the harbour station at Newhaven. This new service catered both for passengers with cars and for those travelling by train, whereas at Dover these remained segregated on separate ships.

With the tall masts but low profile characteristic of French-built ferries of the period, *Villandry* heads out from Newhaven against the background of the rolling Sussex Downs.

MARITIME HERITAGE

6. VIKING INVASION

British Railways may have abandoned its traditional routes from Southampton, but others did not overlook the potential of the city as a cross-Channel ferry port. Its location was convenient for the Midlands, Wales and the West, from which areas Dover and other eastern-Channel ports were a considerable haul before the growth of the motorway network. There was also much easier access from the ports on the other side of the Channel to the holiday regions of Normandy, Brittany, the Loire Valley and the Dordogne. Given the new freedom travellers now had in their motor cars, Paris was no longer the main French destination for British visitors, the basis on which earlier Channel routes had been established, and train services were no longer the principal means of reaching a ferry port.

A Norwegian, Otto Thoresen, recognised these opportunities and, together with his associates, set about the detailed planning of a new service to operate from Southampton to Cherbourg, bringing Scandinavian shipping expertise to the Channel for the first time. Furthermore, just as Stuart Townsend before him had had the foresight to break away from traditional practices in ferry operations, so Thoresen saw yet more possibilities. These new ships would also carry commercial freight vehicles. Many shipping experts at the time felt that it was neither sensible nor feasible to combine the conveyance of passengers and their cars with goods vehicles, but just how far this concept has since developed is obvious to anyone who crosses the Channel today.

There was also another innovation that Thoresen Car Ferries, as it became known, would introduce. Its ships would be the first on the Channel to have 'drive-through' facilities, whereby vehicles would drive aboard through one end of the ship at Southampton, and drive off through the other on reaching France. Without the need to turn round on the car deck, this speeded up the loading and unloading process and hence allowed a considerably faster turn-round at the ports.

With the decision of British Railways to withdraw from Southampton, it was announced that the new Thoresen service would also operate to Le Havre in addition to Cherbourg. Both were important French ports that had historic connections with Southampton. Cherbourg itself is a spacious, sprawling city on the Contentin peninsula, backed by hills and surrounded by pleasant countryside. Le Havre (which means, simply, 'the harbour') is situated at the mouth of the River Seine. It has, in a remarkable example of early town planning, been largely rebuilt following the devastation it suffered during the last war, but it appears today as a collection of rather grey, drab, concrete buildings.

A total of three ships was ordered by Thoresen Car Ferries for these new services from Southampton. With a capacity for 900 passengers and 180 cars, the Norwegian-registered *Viking I* (3,200 gross tons), the first of these revolutionary new vessels, undertook a promotional tour around the British Isles before opening the new route in May 1964, from a newly constructed terminal in Southampton's Outer Dock (later renamed the Princess Alexandra Dock). This, the oldest of the port's docks, had also been the departure point for the previous railway-owned cross-Channel steamers. Today, called Ocean Village and with the ships long gone, it is a yachting and pleasure-boat marina, surrounded by shopping and restaurant facilities, executive housing and offices, but evidence of its earlier use can still be seen.

An identical sister-ship, *Viking II*, joined *Viking I* shortly afterwards, and the similar *Viking III* (built in Germany, unlike her sisters, which had been built in Norway) appeared the following year. They all had the same distinctive colour scheme: a bright orange hull (to be visible in poor weather), a white superstructure (because, said the company, it looked nice) and pale green deck-houses (to reduce sun-glare on open decks). The engine exhaust uptakes, ending in twin, slender funnels, were positioned on each side of the ship, thus allowing a completely unobstructed area on the two vehicle decks, and giving the vessels a very sleek, Scandinavian profile, unlike anything seen on the Channel before.

The latest navigational features were incorporated, including bow thrust units and variable-pitch propellers, which were directly controllable from the bridge. On board the three ships offered bright, spacious accommodation, comfortable lounges, and a high standard of service, including the provision of cabins and 'sleeperettes' for overnight passengers. Norwegian smorgasbord, a novelty at the time for a Channel crossing, was available in one of the restaurants; this Scandinavian cold buffet has since become something of a staple diet on many cross-Channel vessels, yet the British continue to devour it with a lack of subtlety that Scandinavians find most amusing, piling up their plates with an inappropriate mixture of foods, instead of moving selectively through successive helpings of fish, meat, sweets and cheese - and, naturally, with Aquavit and beer to wash down each course.

The new service to Le Havre and Cherbourg quickly established itself as a great success, and a spectacular growth in traffic, covering passengers, private cars and

At Cherbourg in 1964 vehicles leave *Viking II* through the bow doors while foot passengers descend via the gangway at the ship's side. In the foreground arriving British families queue in their Zephyrs, Minxes and Victors, waiting to pass through passport control.

also freight, followed. With this success, such was the pressure for the carriage of freight vehicles on other cross-Channel routes that in 1966 the Dover Harbour Board permitted commercial goods vehicles to be carried on car-ferries from the port for the first time. Today this trade is huge, and most Channel operators find it necessary to augment their passenger car-ferry services with dedicated ferries for road freight.

At Dover, Townsend Car Ferries was also introducing new tonnage on its crossing to Calais, and in 1965 *Free Enterprise II*, the first British-owned drive-through ferry, entered service. Just over 4,000 gross tons, she carried road vehicles on two complete decks, and was the first ship designed to use a new two-tier link-span at Dover, allowing simultaneous loading or unloading on both decks. Over the next decade a further six 'Free Enterprise' ships were to join the company's Dover fleet.

In addition to its sailings to France, Townsend had been seeking to open a new route to Belgium, in competition with the state-owned Belgian Marine Administration. Such a route would provide more direct links with Northern Germany and the Netherlands. Following unsuccessful negotiations with the authorities

at Ostend, arrangements were concluded to use the port of Zeebrugge, further east along the Belgian coast. This had been a tiny seaside village until construction of a new seaport began there towards the end of the last century, protected by a huge, 2½-kilometre mole, curving out from the shore and completed in 1907. Townsend's new Dover-Zeebrugge service commenced in 1966, a 4-hour crossing, and, with an emphasis on freight in addition to the carriage of accompanied cars, it quickly gained support from motorists and road hauliers alike.

Elsewhere others were exploring the possibilities for new cross-Channel routes. In 1965 a little-known Swedish company, Stena Line (named after its founder, Sten A. Olsson), which operated ferry routes in Scandinavia between Sweden and Denmark, announced that it was to start a summer car-ferry service between Tilbury, on the north bank of the Thames opposite Gravesend, and Calais. Highly competitive fares for both passengers and cars were offered, and there was to be just one return sailing a day, with the crossing taking about 5 hours.

The service was known as 'The Londoner' and was aimed not just at people living in the metropolis, but also at those from the Midlands and the North who could avoid the long journey to the Channel coast. During its first season the ship used was the small but attractive *Stena Nordica*. Side-loading and unloading of cars took place at Tilbury Landing Stage, the Port of London's main passenger terminal, whereas stern access was utilised at Calais. The ship was advertised as a 'luxury liner', and the facilities on offer included dining, dancing and a casino. For Londoners wanting a day cruise and a short visit to Calais, the day return fare of £2 9s 6d was a bargain! For passengers travelling further afield but without a car, onward coach connections were provided to Paris.

During the second season the ship operating 'The Londoner' service was the chartered Danish vessel *Prinsessan Christina*, while for the third (and final) summer in 1967, the miniature but nonetheless smart and well-appointed ferry *Stena Baltica* was used. The service was not resumed the following year because, it was said at the time, of the unavailability of a suitable vessel.

With a single small ship, a long crossing, and just one return sailing a day, the impact on cross-Channel passenger numbers was insignificant and the operation cannot have been very profitable. Nevertheless, it was an interesting experiment, and provided the opportunity of reaching France by an unusual route, without the need to venture south of London. Many years later Stena Line, having become in the meantime a very substantial shipping company, was to return to the English Channel with a vengeance, wresting control of newly privatised Sealink from the original purchasers, Sea Containers Ltd. But more of that later.

Following the success of Thoresen Car Ferries at Southampton, the P&O-owned General Steam Navigation Company (GSNC), one of Britain's oldest shipping companies and operators of cargo shipping services to continental ports (and also passenger excursion vessels around the Thames Estuary area), saw its own cross-Channel freight business from Southampton threatened by this Viking invasion. GSNC decided to compete. Forming a subsidiary called Southern Ferries and joining forces with French partners SAGA (Société Anonyme de Gerance et d'Armenent), a new joint enterprise called Normandy Ferries was launched to run passenger and freight services between Southampton and Le Havre. Two new passenger car-ferries, the British-flagged Southern Ferries vessel *Dragon* and the French-flagged SAGA vessel *Leopard*, where built at Nantes and entered service on the route in 1967 and 1968 respectively.

This new venture established P&O, albeit through a subsidiary company, as an operator of short-sea passenger services on the English Channel. Britain's leading shipping group, P&O had been formed in 1837 as the Peninsular & Oriental Steam Navigation Company. It was long-renowned for its passenger liner routes to the Far East and Australia, which were responsible for the introduction into the English language of the word 'posh' ('port outward, starboard home' - for those who could afford a cabin on the shady side of the ship). In addition to its cross-Channel fleet, the group continues to operate cruise, freight and bulk-carrying services worldwide.

The growth in passenger traffic at Southampton stimulated by the new cross-Channel venture (and also by a new route to Spain operated by Swedish Lloyd) was welcome, since the port was beginning a decade that was to see the sudden and rapid decline in the traditional ocean liner services for which it had been renowned since the early years of the century. These had been operated by such legendary shipping lines as Cunard, P&O, Shaw Savill, Royal Mail and Union-Castle, in addition to many

Stena Line of Sweden first appeared on the Channel in 1965 when it began a new seasonal car-ferry service, called 'The Londoner', which operated one return sailing a day between Tilbury, on the River Thames, and Calais, using *Stena Nordica*. The ship had three bars, restaurants and a casino, and offered extremely competitive fares to France for both motorists and foot passengers.

foreign companies whose passenger ships regularly visited the port. It was also possible on many of these ships, especially those in transatlantic service, to make cross-Channel voyages.

The change in fortunes at Southampton was dramatic. While international airlines where experiencing an explosive growth in world-wide travel, long-distance sea travel was declining. It was, however, only Southampton's heavy investment in container-handling facilities that ensured her survival as a major shipping terminal, for eventually her ferry trade, too, was to be lost, transferred to nearby Portsmouth.

At 5,000 gross tons, the sister-ships *Dragon* and *Leopard* introduced at Southampton by Normandy Ferries provided attractively styled accommodation with a wide range of amenities for up to 850 passengers. The vehicle decks, too, were large, with a capacity for 250 cars or a mixture of cars and other vehicles. Although the vessels had only stern-loading facilities, the rear access to the vehicle decks was particularly wide. The ships operated from spacious new terminal buildings on each side of the Channel, separate from Thoresen's own facilities.

With these ships Normandy Ferries also introduced a weekly link between Le Havre and the Irish port of Rosslare, and in an even more ambitious venture began to operate off-season winter sailings from Southampton to Lisbon and Casablanca. This culminated in the ordering of a brand new cruise-ferry, *Eagle*, specifically for running year-round services to Lisbon. Another ship was acquired from Germany, renamed *SF Panther*, and entered service on a further new link from Southampton to San Sebastian, in Spain. However, none of these additional routes proved successful in the long term, and the newer ships were eventually withdrawn. Normandy Ferries returned to just operating *Dragon* and *Leopard* on the cross-Channel service between Southampton and Le Havre.

It used to be the custom, on crossings on the short-sea routes, for passport examination to take place on board the ferry. Passengers were required to visit the passport control office on the ship during the voyage, where they collected a card to hand over on disembarkation, signifying that their passport had been checked. Often they would have to queue, but it was simply regarded as one of the necessary rituals of going abroad. This all changed in 1970, with the opening of a major extension to Dover's car-ferry terminal and the introduction of new boarding and disembarking procedures. Passport control for both inward and outward passengers was then carried out in the terminal, and vehicle processing times were also greatly reduced.

For several years currency restrictions were in force for British travellers, limiting the amount of sterling that could be taken abroad and the value of foreign currency that could be purchased before departure. There were then advantages in sailing on British vessels, as vouchers could be purchased in advance for spending on board, without deduction from the currency allowance. Townsend, to differentiate itself from its Norwegian rivals further down the Channel, made a great feature of this in its ferry brochures, adopting a dominant 'buy British' theme (but omitting to mention that every vessel in the 'Free Enterprise' fleet had been built abroad).

By the late 1960s competition on the Channel was intensifying. In order to strengthen its operations and gain the benefits in efficiency that came with size, Townsend (based at Dover and competing with the nationalised British and French railway-owned services) entered discussions with Thoresen (based at Southampton and now competing with Normandy Ferries), with a view to merging their respective ferry fleets. After due consideration this was agreed, and in 1968 George Nott Industries, the owners of Townsend Car Ferries, purchased the share capital of Thoresen Car Ferries to form the European Ferries Group and become the UK's largest independent ferry concern. The new combined operation was styled 'Townsend Thoresen', and the Thoresen orange hull was subsequently adopted for the entire fleet. Thus the company that was to play a dominant role in UK ferry operations for almost 20 years was born. Three years later the European Ferries Group expanded further by purchasing the Transport Ferry Service of the Atlantic Steam Navigation Company, adding routes from Felixstowe to

Townsend's 'buy British' appeal in 1967 would seem to have been something of a lost cause amongst those who had already opted to spend their holidays abroad. Nevertheless, passengers could conserve the very limited currency allowances then in force by using vouchers ordered in advance for purchases on board these British-registered ships.

the Low Countries and from Preston and Cairnryan to Northern Ireland to Townsend Thoresen's well-established English Channel services.

After the railways had been nationalised in 1948 and British Railways created, the railway-owned ships had been placed under the operational control of the respective BR Region. In the case of English Channel services this was the Southern Region, whose rail network, the most extensively worked in the world, stretched from Weymouth in the west to Broadstairs in the east. (For the first few months of nationalisation, however, Channel Island services from Weymouth continued to be run by the Western Region, successors to the Great Western Railway, whose ships they acquired.)

Then in 1963 the extensive British Railways shipping fleet, covering routes across the Irish Sea, the English Channel and the North Sea, together with domestic services (such as those to the Isle of Wight) and the ownership of several ports, including the Channel ports of Newhaven and Folkestone, became centrally managed under the Shipping and International Services Division of

BR. In the early 1970s the fleet name 'Sealink' was adopted, to encompass both British Railways' own ships and
those operated in partnership with BR by the nationalised
ferry concerns of Belgium, France and the Netherlands.

By now the only cross-Channel ferry port serving France
that had no car-ferry sailings was Folkestone. Traditional
passenger ships sailing to Calais and Boulogne still provided the only service from here, but the facilities available at
Folkestone Harbour for embarking travellers were becoming woefully run-down. One of the earliest packet ports to
commence regular steamship services to the Continent was
to be the last to be adapted for the ubiquitous symbol of
the 20th century, the motor car. Faced with the prospect of
either closing down the Kent port and the services that
operated from it, or transforming it into the base for a
modern car-ferry operation, British Railways, the port's
owner, decided on an investment programme that would
modernise and upgrade the harbour facilities and provide
two purpose-built passenger car-ferries for the service to
Boulogne. A new passenger terminal was built adjacent to
Folkestone Harbour station, vehicle handling areas were
constructed, and a vehicle loading ramp provided at the
inward end of the port's massive stone pier.

Below Old and new at Folkestone Harbour. Berthed at the end of
the pier is the traditional mail steamer *Maid of Orleans*, while at
the newly completed car-ferry terminal is *Hengist*, one of a pair of
new vessels introduced on the Folkestone-Boulogne service in
1972. *Hengist* and her sister *Horsa* were the first vessels to carry
the newly adopted fleet name of 'Sealink'. Folkestone was the last
of the cross-Channel railway ports to be adapted for car-ferry
operations, a move that was to lead to the end of all conventional
passenger ships on the Channel.

The new ships, named *Hengist* and *Horsa* after the legendary brothers who landed on the Isle of Thanet in 449 to help King Vortigern against the Picts, were built in Brest and entered service between Folkestone and Boulogne in 1972. These solid-looking vessels, designed, unlike Dover-based car-ferries, to carry both car passengers and those travelling by train, introduced several innovations in the range of passenger facilities provided, and a brighter, more modern atmosphere was created on board. With the establishment of the new Sealink consortium they were the first ships to have the brand name painted along their sides. A third vessel of this type was also built at Brest, and joined the longer Newhaven-Dieppe route in 1973 as *Senlac*, running alongside the French ferries *Villandry* and *Valancay*, and displacing the converted *Falaise*.

Falaise was moved westwards to open car-ferry sailings from Weymouth to the Channel Islands, but was soon replaced on this route by a newly acquired Swedish ship, *Svea Drott*, which was given the name *Earl Godwin*. A service from Weymouth to Cherbourg was also initiated, and Sealink transferred *Maid of Kent* from Dover to operate on this new route.

Two new vessels of much-advanced design and intended, like those at Folkestone and Newhaven, for carrying both car and foot passengers, joined the RMT's Dover to Ostend service in 1973 and 1974. *Prins Phillipe* and *Prince Laurent* were the first Belgian drive-through ships, but had a rather harsher profile than previous Ostend ferries, and lacked the traditionally elegant lines associated with this company.

The remaining conventional mail-ships in the cross-Channel trade were now serving out their notice. The segregation between foot passengers and those with cars, still prevalent on the short-sea routes, no longer made sense. The future would lie with combined passenger and vehicle ferries. Dover, however, was at a disadvantage, since conventional rail-connected sailings were based in the Western Docks at the Admiralty Pier, which had its own Marine railway station for boat-trains but was more than a mile from the car-ferry terminal in the Eastern Docks, at the other side of the harbour. To allow for the operation of combined sailings by the newer breed of multi-purpose ships, a new vehicle ferry berth was opened at the Admiralty Pier in 1974. Car-ferry sailings to both Calais and Ostend were introduced from here, with boat-train connections for foot passengers. These new services ran in addition to the normal car-ferry sailings operating out of the Eastern Docks.

Viking I, the first 'drive-through' ferry in cross-Channel service, in the Outer Dock at Southampton in 1969, showing the large vehicle deck that allowed commercial freight vehicles to be carried for the first time on a passenger vessel. The low glass-fronted building on the right is the Thoresen passenger terminal, now replaced by modern apartments as part of Southampton's Ocean Village development. The dockside building on the left was used by the earlier railway-owned services across the Channel, but is now the site of Canute's Pavilion, a shopping and restaurant mall. The dock itself has become a yachting marina and a base for local excursion vessels.

MARITIME HERITAGE

Right Viking I on passage from Southampton to Cherbourg. Accompanied by siren blasts, her Norwegian ensign is lowered in an exchange of salutes with *Viking II*, from which this photograph was taken, as the two ships pass in mid-Channel.

Right Viking II at Southampton in 1970. In the foreground is the bow of *Viking IV*, a freight-ferry introduced by Thoresen to augment the commercial vehicle capacity of its three passenger ships.

Below Viking II approaching her berth at Cherbourg, with the French courtesy flag fluttering from her foremast.

Left *Viking III* in dry dock in 1972, showing the open bow door and the lowered internal loading ramp, as painters touch up her loading marks. The position of the bow thruster can be seen below the waterline.

Right Townsend Ferries' second new ship, *Free Enterprise II*, the first British-owned drive-through ferry, is seen here arriving at Calais in 1975 following the 1968 merger between Townsend and Thoresen.

Right *Free Enterprise III* approaches the link-span at Calais, with *Vortigern* berthed behind.

Below *Free Enterprise IV* was transferred from Dover to assist at Southampton. She is seen here in Southampton's Outer Dock early in the New Year of 1970, still in her original Townsend colours. The traditional nautical Christmas tree adorns her foremast.

Above In 1966 Townsend Ferries opened a new route into Belgium between Dover and Zeebrugge. *Free Enterprise VI* arrives in Zeebrugge Harbour in 1978 with the orange hull of Townsend Thoresen, but as with all the former Townsend ships still carries the single name of Townsend on the superstructure forward of the funnel.

Below In 1967 no more than £15 in sterling per passenger and up to £50 in travellers cheques or foreign currency could be taken out of the country, plus an additional £25 for those taking a car abroad. In spite of these disincentives against foreign travel, however, Townsend was already operating up to 24 sailings a day from Dover at peak periods. Further savings on foreign expenditure were offered by the ferry company through a food-hamper scheme, whereby supplies ordered in advance could be collected at Dover before departure, and Townsend also operated a camping equipment hire facility and a motorists mail-order service, all adding to the company's claim to be the 'Friendly Free Enterprise Line'.

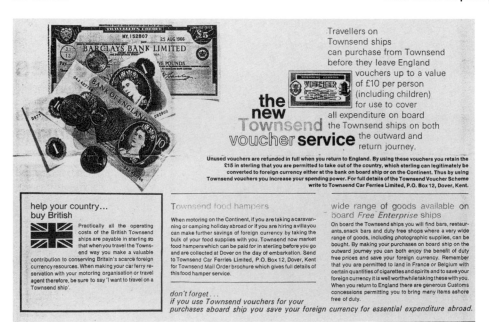

Above right *Free Enterprise VII* at the car-ferry terminal in Dover's Eastern Docks in 1975.

Right *Free Enterprise VIII* speeding past the White Cliffs as she approaches Dover at the end of a 4-hour crossing from Zeebrugge, also in 1975.

Above For the 1966 season Stena Line introduced the chartered Danish vessel *Prinsessan Christina* on its 'Londoner' service. She is seen here at Calais in that year, at the end of her 5-hour voyage that has taken her down the River Thames, out through the Estuary and around the Kent Coast, certainly an interesting way of reaching France.

Below The small but well-appointed vessel *Stena Baltica*, in the third and final year of 'The Londoner' service, berthed at Calais in 1967. No one would have imagined then that Stena Line would later become one of the major operators on the Channel and the largest ferry company in the world. There was, however, a 23-year gap before Stena returned to these waters.

Above The sleek lines of Normandy Ferries' brand new UK-registered ship *Dragon* at the company's terminal in Le Havre. Built in 1967, she was the first of a pair of identical vessels introduced by the newly formed Anglo-French company to compete with Thoresen Car Ferries on its route between the French port and Southampton.

Right The wide stern door of *Dragon* seen from the link-span at the Normandy Ferries' terminal at Le Havre in 1967.

Right *Dragon*'s sister-ship, the French-flagged *Leopard*, sailing up Southampton Water at the end of an overnight crossing from Le Havre in 1979. A distinctive light-blue hull has replaced the earlier all-white colour scheme of these vessels.

Above *Hengist* arrives at Folkestone in 1974, and turns off the pier to back up to the link-span. Most drive-through ferries used stern loading in Britain and bow loading in France.

Below Similar in design to *Hengist* and *Horsa*, *Senlac* was introduced in 1973 to provide increased capacity on the Newhaven-Dieppe route, and is seen here across the yachts moored in Newhaven harbour in 1975. *Senlac*'s funnel carries the house-flag that was unique to the joint Anglo-French operation on this route, rather than the double-arrow logo then adopted on all other British Sealink ships.

MARITIME HERITAGE

Above Two advanced new ships were introduced by the Belgian state-owned RMT company on its Dover-Ostend service in the early 1970s. They were the first Belgian drive-through ferries, and *Prince Laurent*, seen here leaving Dover in 1979, was also the first ship to use a new car-ferry link-span at the port's Admiralty Pier, adjacent to the Marine station. This allowed both car passengers and those travelling by train to be carried on the same vessel, which had not hitherto been the practice at Dover, where the mail-ship berths and the car-ferry terminal were located at opposite sides of the harbour, some 2 miles apart.

Below Prins Philippe, sister-ship to *Prince Laurent*, arrives at her home port of Ostend in 1978. Both vessels were equipped with an experimental computer navigation system, the forerunner of what was subsequently adopted universally on all cross-Channel ferries.

7. ON THE CREST OF A WAVE

The quest for increased speed across the Channel was eagerly pursued by Victorian engineers as they sought improvements to the power and efficiency of marine propulsion systems. Many technical innovations and new engineering developments were first applied on the Channel before being more widely utilised elsewhere. As with the Atlantic, record crossings of the Channel gave ship operators a significant marketing edge over their competitors. In recent decades, however, there has been no general increase in the passage times of cross-Channel ships; indeed, on the shortest routes today, most crossings by conventional ferry are slower than the fastest times available in the earlier part of the century.

The main reason for this has been competition from the air. The arrival of air travel provided a means of transport with which the shipping companies could obviously not hope to compete on speed, and we have already seen how much of the passenger traffic between London and Paris has been captured by the airlines.

The first pioneering flight across the English Channel was undertaken by Louis Blériot in the early hours of 25 July 1909. He undertook this heroic crossing in a 24 hp monoplane, taking off before dawn from a site just west of Calais and landing, unexpected and unseen by anyone except the local policeman, close to Dover Castle. As news of Blériot's feat spread throughout the town, he was given a hero's welcome.

Regular passenger air services between London and Paris commenced in 1919. Air transport even began to enter the cross-Channel car-carrying business when, in 1948, Silver City Airways started a service conveying accompanied cars across to France from Lympne Airport (and also, later, from Lydd) in Kent, using Bristol Super freighters carrying three cars and 12 passengers. Services were subsequently extended to Ostend and Cherbourg. In 1954 a rival concern, Channel Air Bridge, began operations from Southend to Basle and Geneva, using converted DC4s that could carry five cars and 23 passengers. The two companies eventually amalgamated to form British United Air Ferries (later renamed British Air Ferries), and concentrated their services on Southend. However, rising fuel costs and the very limited capacity of these specially adapted aircraft meant that this did not remain an economically viable venture, and the services were discontinued in the 1970s.

Another important reason, in addition to air competition, why the design speed of conventional ships has not increased significantly is the huge cost penalty introduced in terms of the propulsion unit needed and the amount of fuel consumed. For a ship to move forward by its own length, a quantity of water equal to the ship's weight must be moved aside. The faster this is done, the more energy it takes, and as ship speed increases, so each extra knot (nautical mile per hour) requires progressively more additional power. A doubling of engine power (and a consequent doubling of fuel consumption) produces far less than a doubling of speed. In the harsh economics of modern ferry operation, therefore, speed is a compromise that has to be made between the additional costs incurred and the extra income likely to be generated. For a conventional cross-Channel ferry, the answer comes out at about 20 knots. A fast turn-round in port is also important, of course, to maximise the number of crossings each vessel can make.

But the earlier nautical engineers did realise that there were other ways of increasing speed beyond a simple increase in power. Since the majority of this power is consumed by moving water aside, it was realised that if only the bulk of the ship's hull could be lifted clear of the water, most of this resistance would be gone and considerably less power would then be needed to move the vessel forward. Quite how this might be achieved on a practical scale was not, however, clear.

A British engineer, Christopher Cockerell, came up with a possible answer. He began experimenting at home in the early 1950s with various household items, including a vacuum cleaner and a pair of kitchen scales. Next, he carried out a more elaborate practical test of his idea at Oulton Broad in Suffolk. Eventually he won the financial backing of the NRDC (the now defunct National Research Development Corporation) to support his new invention, which he christened the hovercraft. Cockerell had realised that if a craft is supported on a cushion of air, most of the resistance between it and the water over which it hovers has gone. Furthermore, such a craft can equally well travel over flat land, and is therefore truly amphibious.

An experimental craft, the SRN1, was built by aircraft manufacturer Saunders Roe and had its first 'flight' at East Cowes on the Isle of Wight in 1959 (the initials stood for 'Saunders Roe Number 1'). The hovercraft was regarded as an extension of aeronautical technology rather than of marine engineering, and was therefore registered as an aircraft, even though it never got more than a couple of feet off the ground. Later in the same year, on 25 July, the 50th anniversary of the first flight across the Channel by Louis Blériot, SRN1 made its first historic crossing of the English Channel from Calais to Dover, completing the journey in 2 hours. It would have been quicker by ferry, but at least the technical feasibility of the hovercraft had been demonstrated. But whether this was to be just a passing novelty or the beginning of a transport revolution was not yet clear; certainly the strange-looking craft, resembling a cotton reel on top of an up-turned dinner plate, seemed an odd contender to compete with established shipping services.

Over the next few years a number of more advanced passenger-carrying hovercraft were built by both Vickers and by Westland Aircraft, who had taken over Saunders Roe, and these were operated commercially on trial routes in the North West of England, in the Bristol Channel and across the Solent. With initial success demonstrated, notwithstanding the occurrence of a few breakdowns and occasional weather problems, the hovercraft interests of the two manufacturers were merged in 1966 to become the Isle of Wight-based British Hovercraft Corporation.

Cross-Channel operations began in 1966 between the harbours of Ramsgate and Calais, using two SRN6 hovercraft carrying 36 passengers. The service was run by a new Swedish-owned company, Hoverlloyd Ltd, formed jointly by Swedish Lloyd (then operators of ferries across the North Sea and between the UK and Spain) and Swedish America Line (a transatlantic shipping company). Although the inaugural crossing had to be cancelled due to waves in the Channel in excess of 6 feet, the company was determined to succeed in this venture, and planned to introduce larger car-carrying craft. In the same year

Townsend Car Ferries introduced a cross-Channel passenger service using an SRN6 craft to run between Dover and Calais, but were not impressed with its reliability and withdrew completely from further hovercraft operation.

In 1968 the world's first car-carrying hovercraft, the new Mountbatten Class SRN4, named *The Princess Margaret* (who, with her husband Lord Snowdon, travelled on the inaugural crossing), was introduced by Seaspeed, the hovercraft division established by British Railways. This new craft could carry 30 cars and 250 passengers, and made the crossing between Dover's Eastern Docks and a new hoverport at Le Portel, near Boulogne, in 35 minutes at a speed of 50 knots. The following year a similar service to Calais, using a new hoverport close to the French port's car-ferry facilities, was started by Hoverlloyd from a new terminal at Pegwell Bay, near Ramsgate, using two SRN4 craft called *Swift* and *Sure*. This slightly longer crossing took 40 minutes. Another craft, *The Princess Anne*, also joined Seaspeed. There were ambitious plans to develop new routes elsewhere and even to construct much larger craft for transatlantic

A new name, a new look and a new sound on the Channel. Hoverlloyd's SRN4 hovercraft *Sir Christopher*, named in honour of its inventor, makes an impressive sight and an impressive noise as it approaches the slipway. Combining aeronautical technology with marine engineering, hovercraft became a familiar sight in the Channel and carried a significant proportion of the total traffic on the short-sea routes. In spite of their initial success, however, the English Channel remained the only place in the world where car-carrying hovercraft were operated commercially.

operation, but the cross-Channel service has remained ever since the only route in the world on which car-carrying hovercraft have been used.

These early crossings were not without their problems. The flexible skirt fixed around the base of each craft to contain the air cushion was a frequent cause of trouble until design modifications were introduced. The loss of a propeller at Pegwell Bay on one occasion caused all hovercraft to be temporarily grounded while checks were carried out. Adverse weather, too, was often a cause of cancelled crossings. Nevertheless, with a commitment to succeed and the pioneering spirit needed for all such new undertakings, hovercraft became firmly established as an alternative way to cross the Channel, carrying both accompanied cars and foot passengers. They were a particular favourite with those who preferred to get the crossing over quickly!

Two more type SRN4 hovercraft, *Sir Christopher* (named after the now knighted inventor) and *The Prince of Wales*, later joined Hoverlloyd's Ramsgate-based fleet. Meanwhile two car-carrying hovercraft of French design were under construction for SNCF to operate to Dover.

With the cancellation of work on the Channel Tunnel, Seaspeed decided to have its two existing craft lengthened to increase capacity to 54 cars and almost 400 passengers. With these developments in hand, Dover Harbour Board agreed to construct a new larger hoverport at the western side of the harbour, adjacent to the Prince of Wales Pier. This opened in 1978, although a direct rail link to the new terminal that had been planned never materialised. Unfortunately, the first of the new French hovercraft, or Naviplanes as they were called, was destroyed by fire before entering service. The second, the *Ingenieur Jean Bertin*, named after its designer (who may have wished that he had remained anonymous), proved so unreliable that it was broken up a few years later.

Although hovercraft succeeded in overcoming water resistance and could thus attain high speeds, considerable power was still needed to lift the craft from the surface, so fuel consumption was high and profitability, at best, was marginal. Using gas-turbine aircraft engines, they were also extremely noisy. Furthermore, the amphibious nature of these craft, an advantage exploited in hovercraft operations elsewhere in the world, was not a particular benefit in cross-Channel service, where sophisticated harbour facilities existed on both sides of the Channel, with deep water between them. By 1980 Hoverlloyd and Seaspeed had, between them, succeeded in capturing about one-fifth of the total cross-Channel market, but had won very little share in the profits. Clearly, high-speed travel across the sea had an appeal, but operators began to look at other ways of providing it.

One alternative was the hydrofoil. This is a vessel that uses underwater foils or 'wings' beneath the hull to provide lift as speed increases, in much the same way as the wings of an aircraft allow it to take off from the ground. At speed, therefore, these foils raise the hull of the vessel out of the water. This principle was first tried on an experimental scale in 1906, but only commercially developed some 50 years later. The hydrofoil is inherently more efficient and potentially quieter than the hovercraft. During the 1960s both Italy and the Soviet Union began

Advertising a new way to cross the Channel that was fast, cheap, fun, easy . . . and British, Seaspeed introduced the travelling public to its 35-minute car-carrying hovercraft crossings to Boulogne. With great hyperbole it promised 'an adventure for the family, a first photo for the holiday album even your great grandchildren will be proud of'.

building a number of passenger-carrying hydrofoil craft, which mostly had fixed, angled 'skis' attached to the hull, and used conventional screw propulsion. Such vessels have been used on the Thames, on Isle of Wight services, and in the Channel Islands.

A larger type of craft was later introduced by the American aircraft manufacturer Boeing. Using its aeronautical expertise, it developed an advanced computer-controlled hydrofoil with adjustable, fully submerged, horizontal foils. Propulsion was by means of water jets, and over 250 passengers could be carried in aircraft-type cabins on two decks at a speed in excess of 40 knots. Called the Jetfoil, these craft have been in service on a number of routes around the world since 1975.

A temporary Jetfoil service, using a Boeing craft called *Flying Princess*, was initiated by P&O across the Channel from London in 1977. Two years later a company called Seajet began a service between Brighton Marina and Dieppe using a Jetfoil named *Normandy Princess*. The crossing time was 2 hours, and through connections (by coach in England and by train in France) were offered between London and Paris. For a supplementary fee, passengers could travel in the 'Captain's Cabin', a secluded

A new Hoverport was opened at Dover in 1978, built on reclaimed land in the Western Docks against the Prince of Wales Pier and including an impressive airport-style passenger terminal. Three SRN4 hovercraft can be seen here, one arriving on the slipway and two parked on the apron (the craft on the left is undergoing maintenance work).

area forward on the main deck, and partake of champagne and light refreshments. Others requiring sustenance on the crossing had to plan ahead and purchase meal trays in the terminal before departure.

In 1980, following the success of its earlier trial, P&O Jet Ferries was established to operate a two-craft service with *Jetferry One* and *Jetferry Two* between London (from a base on the Thames near St Katherine's Dock, just below Tower Bridge) and Ostend. The journey time was about 3½ hours, and an on-board service of drinks and complimentary refreshments was provided. It was felt that a direct service from the heart of London, close to the City, to the rail terminal at Ostend, with onward train connections to Brussels, Northern Germany and the Netherlands, would appeal in particular to business travellers. Passenger numbers never came up to expectations, however, probably because the journey time was too long to compete with air travel, and after just seven months the service closed. The Seajet route from

Calling it 'the ship that flies' and denoting sailings by 'flight number', in 1979 Seajet introduced a Boeing Jetfoil on a new cross-Channel route between Brighton Marina and Dieppe (with through connections linking London and Paris), using a craft named *Normandy Princess*. It was not a commercial success, and more recent attempts to operate high-speed Channel crossings from Brighton have also failed.

BRIGHTON-DIEPPE
SEAJET
LONDON-PARIS
4th EDITION   FROM 30 SEPTEMBER, 1979.

Brighton also came to an end at much the same time. This, too, had suffered from insufficient passenger numbers, while the additional problem of a port blockade at Dieppe during the French fishermen's dispute of 1980 (a perennial cause of disrupted ferry services) did nothing to help.

The Belgian authorities had also been considering high-speed services on their traditional route between Ostend and Dover. The possibilities of using hovercraft had been examined, and one of the Seaspeed SRN4s did make an exploratory visit to Ostend. RMT, the Belgian Marine Administration, settled instead for a passenger-only service using Boeing Jetfoils, and two such craft, *Princesse Clementine* and *Prinses Stephanie* (note again the two languages adopted) joined the route in 1981, with a crossing time of 100 minutes. At Dover the Jetfoils operated from a berth adjacent to Dover Marine station, and connecting rail services were run to and from Victoria, with a check-in lounge for the exclusive use of Jetfoil passengers at the London terminus.

With the need to promote and maintain a high standard of service on this route, a Jetfoil lounge was also opened at Ostend, but rather better terminal facilities than were available at Dover's ageing Marine station were needed. RMT adopted the unique solution of converting one of its earlier Dover-Ostend mail-ships, *Reine Astrid*, withdrawn from service in 1981, into a floating Jetfoil terminal, to be permanently moored alongside Admiralty Pier, with lounge, check-in and customs facilities all located on board. A direct walkway linking it with Dover Marine station (later renamed Dover Western Docks) was provided.

The Dover-Ostend Jetfoil service rapidly gained in popularity and, undergoing many changes in livery (as with the parallel Belgian car-ferry service), eventually transferred its English base from Dover to Ramsgate. The floating terminal came into its own here, for after being towed to Vlissingen (Flushing) for inspection and modification, it was simply relocated at Ramsgate. Train connections continued to operate, with a bus link between Ramsgate station and the port.

On the hovercraft front, meanwhile, both Hoverlloyd and Seaspeed recognised that salvation and long-term profitability could only come from an amalgamation of the two companies and a rationalisation of their joint services. Following lengthy discussions the merger was eventually agreed, and in 1981 the new combined company, called Hoverspeed, was established. Services were concentrated on Dover, with Ramsgate Hoverport at Pegwell Bay initially retained as a maintenance base until its complete closure a few years later. The terminal building at Pegwell, which used to boast a bar and dance-floor with live music for waiting passengers and local residents alike, stood for a number of years, neglected and van-

The Viking ship at Pegwell Bay, a gift from Denmark that made a commemorative sailing across the North Sea to Kent in 1949, overlooks a more recent form of transport at Ramsgate Hoverport in 1975. The terminal building had a viewing gallery on the roof from which the arrival and departure of the hovercraft could be observed. The Viking ship is still there but not so the hoverport, which closed after Hoverlloyd amalgamated with Seaspeed in 1981 and all hovercraft services were transferred to Dover.

dalised, a monument to a transport innovation that didn't quite start a revolution. It was eventually demolished.

Three years after its creation, Hoverspeed underwent a management buy-out, breaking away from its founding companies. In 1986 it was sold again, this time to Sea Containers of Bermuda, whose President, James Sherwood, realised that the future of fast Channel ferries lay with wave-piercing catamarans, then undergoing development, and not with hovercraft. Dover's fleet of hovercraft was gradually reduced (some being cannibalised to provide spares for the others) until only the two 'stretched' craft, *The Princess Margaret* and *The Princess Anne*, remained in service, pending replacement by the new catamarans. Boulogne Hoverport was closed, and just the single route between Dover and Calais was maintained.

The concept of a catamaran or twin-hulled vessel is not new; indeed, such craft built of logs were first used centuries ago in South America. Nor does it utilise the principles of the hovercraft or the hydrofoil in lifting the hull out of the water to reduce resistance. Catamarans are conventional displacement vessels, and like any ship they continue, at speed, to displace their own weight of water a la Archimedes. Their increased performance capability, however, often exploited in the yachting world, comes from the design of the slender twin outer hulls, which make it much easier to push aside the water as the vessel moves forward. We have already seen, in Chapter 2, the Victorian attempts to exploit this idea in cross-Channel service. Now this technology was being considerably advanced by new developments being pursued by International Catamarans of Tasmania.

The first Australian catamarans to operate in Britain were two passenger-only craft introduced in 1986 across the Solent between Ryde and Portsmouth, a route also owned by Sea Containers. This company then placed orders for larger, car-carrying versions for operation by Hoverspeed across the Channel. These 26-metre-long SeaCats would have a capacity for 450 passengers and up to 90 cars, with a speed of 40 knots, twice that of a conventional ferry. The design incorporated a third central hull (not normally in contact with the water in calm conditions) which gives added buoyancy in rough weather. Unlike the hovercraft or Jetfoil, where passengers had to remain seated, here they could wander around over two decks to visit the on-board cafe and bar and the duty-free shop, and even step outside on to the after deck, an exhilarating experience as the vessel speeds across the Channel.

The first of these SeaCats to be delivered was *Hoverspeed Great Britain*. She sailed under her own power from Australia, crossing the Pacific to South America and on to the United States. On the final leg of her journey from New York she broke the Blue Riband record for the fastest crossing of the Atlantic Ocean by a passenger vessel. Hitherto this had been held by the American liner *United States*, which had crossed the Atlantic in just under 3½ days on her maiden voyage in 1952. *Hoverspeed Great Britain* managed to clip almost 3 hours off this record to claim the once-coveted Hales Trophy, held previously by such illustrious liners as *Mauretania*, *Normandie* and *Queen Mary*. The SeaCat crossing was undoubtedly a magnificent achievement, and received plenty of much-deserved publicity. But with no passengers on board (and with no capability for carrying any on such a long voyage), it was hardly in the traditional spirit of the Blue Riband.

The intention was to put the *Hoverspeed Great Britain* on the Dover-Calais route, but due to difficulties in completing arrangements at Dover, she started service instead between Portsmouth and Cherbourg, in August 1990. This was unfortunate, because the longer crossing (2½ hours) made it more difficult to overcome the inevitable teething troubles of such an innovative new vessel, and also gave the passengers longer to suffer the effects of sea-sickness that the unaccustomed motion of the SeaCat seemed prone to cause. Furthermore, the vessel's introduction had been delayed by problems in obtaining a passenger certificate from the Department of Transport, which insisted on modifications to the craft before commercial operation could commence. The media attention given to this inauspicious start severely dented the SeaCat's image created by the record-breaking Atlantic crossing. Improvements to the propulsion system were, however, effected and the trim of the vessel modified, and in October Hoverspeed was able to announce that a reliable service was being maintained 'with a high degree of passenger satisfaction'.

A second SeaCat, *Hoverspeed France*, reaching Britain by way of the Suez Canal, joined Hoverspeed, which terminated its Cherbourg service and in the summer of 1991 began crossings from Dover, operating from the Eastern Docks to Calais and Boulogne. The following year, with the ending of conventional ferry services between Folkestone and Boulogne, Hoverspeed placed its third new SeaCat, *Hoverspeed Boulogne*, on this route. Speeded up rail connections between London and Paris via Folkestone and Boulogne were introduced at the same time, and this service also provided the Channel link for Sea Containers' luxury Venice-Simplon Orient Express, certainly offering contrasting styles in travel!

Since then, other Australian-built craft have joined the company, but all have been interchanged with other high-speed services operated by Sea Containers, including those across the Irish Sea, in Scandinavia, and in Australia. Because of this pressure to develop new routes, Hoverspeed has been obliged to retain its two elderly hovercraft in service from Dover longer than anticipated, and in consequence has refurbished them to ensure continued operation for several more years. In order to get closer integration of SeaCat and hovercraft services, SeaCat operation was switched to a new facility at Dover's International Hoverport in the Western Docks, and the names of SeaCats now in operation across the

Dover Strait, such as *SeaCat Calais* and *SeaCat Boulogne*, acknowledge that this is the age of the wave-piercer.

But although the hovercraft era may be drawing to a close, the two remaining craft continue to provide the fastest cross-Channel service available, carrying cars and passengers across to France in less time than is possible through the tunnel. Indeed, in 1995 *The Princess Anne* established a new Channel record by crossing from Dover to Calais in just 22 minutes.

During 1990 a smaller, British-built, passenger-carrying wave-piercing catamaran, *Condor 9*, was introduced on the cross-Channel route between Weymouth, the Channel Islands and St Malo by Condor Ferries, operators of fast-ferry services in the Channel Islands and from there to France. However, this, too, suffered technical problems and was withdrawn for modifications. Plans for operating larger Australian-built craft from Weymouth were delayed, but eventually the passenger and car-carrying SeaCat *Condor 10* was introduced on the Channel Islands route in 1993, with a capacity for 600 passengers and 80 cars. This was replaced by the larger *Condor 11* in 1995, and in 1996 by *Condor 12*, a new 86-metre SeaCat capable of carrying 800 passengers and 200 cars.

In 1992 a French-designed catamaran, operated by Advanced Channel Express, ran experimental passenger sailings linking Brighton Marina with Fecamp and Dieppe. A similar service, using a Norwegian-built craft, was operated to Fecamp during 1995 by the newly established Brighton Ferries, but following losses this company was wound up.

In spite of the hesitant start of wave-piercing catamarans, they have now become well-established on a number of routes around Britain, and new craft, so-called Super SeaCats, carrying even more passengers and cars, and arranged on an open-plan system enabling passengers to circulate on board more freely, have been introduced. Hoverspeed has built up a considerable level of new business, and has established a 'Premier' service (akin to airline Business Class). The parent company, Sea Containers, has purchased larger SeaCats from Austral Ships Pty, another Australian-based manufacturer of catamarans, for operation on a number of routes world-wide. These new craft can, for the first time, handle coaches in addition to private cars.

Other operators, too, have brought advanced vessels of this type into cross-Channel service. Stena Line has introduced its Stena Lynx SeaCats on the English Channel, as well as a chartered single-hulled high-speed craft, *Stena Pegasus*, which crossed between Newhaven and Dieppe in just 2 hours, half the time of a conventional ferry. Others are considering the use of these new fast ferries, and SeaCats are being introduced between Ramsgate and Ostend by a new company that has taken over the route from RMT.

Global voyages by SeaCats have also become more routine, both for the delivery of new craft and for the regular transfer of vessels between the northern and southern hemispheres to operate seasonal summer services. Such has been the growth in the opening of new routes that it has sometimes proved difficult to match demand with the available supply of SeaCats.

But a glimpse into the future of ferry operations is per-

MARITIME HERITAGE

haps most clearly seen in developments recently undertaken by Stena Line. Three large, revolutionary, twin-hulled HSS (High-Speed Ship) craft have been built by Finnyards shipbuilders in Finland for operation from UK ports across the Irish Sea, the North Sea, and the English Channel. These futuristic-looking, streamlined vessels carry 1,500 passengers and up to 375 cars at speeds of up to 40 knots. With an open-plan passenger deck incorporating spacious lounge areas, bars, food court, restaurant and shopping facilities, they combine the ambience of a modern luxury ferry with a doubling of speed compared with existing ships. But apart from two small 'fresh air galleries' at the stern, passengers are cocooned inside in air-conditioned comfort. A bracing stroll on deck in the face of a stiff Channel breeze will, unfortunately, become a thing of the past.

Clearly, though, the development of this new fast-ferry technology has only just begun, and it remains to be seen how well it can take on the challenge of the Channel Tunnel during the 21st century.

The first car-carrying hovercraft, *The Princess Margaret*, arrives at Dover's original hoverport, which opened in 1968. This was located in the Eastern Docks as an integral part of the car-ferry terminal.

Cars unload from *The Princess Margaret* through the stern while coaches await to take foot passengers to passport control and customs examination, and on to the town's railway station.

MARITIME HERITAGE

Opposite page Having been enlarged to increase carrying capacity to almost 400 passengers and 54 cars by the insertion of a new mid-section, the Seaspeed SRN super-4 hovercraft *The Princess Anne* roars past Dover's Prince of Wales Pier towards the hoverport in 1979. Upon arrival (*below*) passengers are escorted to the terminal building by a Seaspeed stewardess, while on the right a road-tanker refuels the hovercraft.

Right The French-built N500 hovercraft *Ingenieur Jean Bertin* leaving Dover, also in 1979. Stylish in design but unreliable in operation, it was scrapped after only a short time in service. Unlike the British craft, the N500 design, of which *Ingenieur Jean Bertin* was the only example to be completed, had two decks, with passenger accommodation located on the upper level.

Right The apron at Dover Hoverport showing the rear of two craft in the colours of Hoverspeed, a company formed in 1981 by the merger of Dover-based Seaspeed with Ramsgate-based Hoverlloyd. The internal single-deck layout of these craft, having a large drive-through vehicle deck with passenger accommodation in two separate seating areas along each side, can be clearly seen in this 1990 view.

Right A Hoverspeed craft heads out of Dover soon after the merged company was formed, when crossings were maintained initially from both Dover and Ramsgate. It wasn't long, however, before services were concentrated at Dover and the hoverport at Ramsgate was closed.

The P&O Jetfoil *Flying Princess* approaching Gravesend as she speeds up the River Thames towards London on an experimental service from Belgium that was operated in 1977.

The Sealink Jetfoil *Prinses Stephanie*, one of a pair operated by the Belgian company RMT between Dover and Ostend, passes the circular Lighthouse Café at the end of Dover's Prince of Wales Pier in 1985. This café, a popular venue from which to observe the passing shipping scene, was badly damaged by storms and has since been replaced by another building sited on the landward side of the lighthouse in a less exposed position.

Dropping into the water as she reduces speed, *Prinses Stephanie* arrives in Ostend Harbour and heads towards the berth alongside the railway station, from where her passengers will be conveyed by connecting train to Brussels.

Opposite page Carrying the company's new name following the transfer of its English terminal from Dover to Ramsgate, Oostende Line's Jetfoil *Princesse Clementine* is seen at speed in mid-Channel, and rounding the Eastern breakwater at Ramsgate.

MARITIME HERITAGE

tering from other operators. These included *Cornouailles* (3,400 tons) and *Prince of Brittany* (5,500 tons), a Swedish-owned vessel that had previously been operating in Canada. In addition to the Plymouth-Roscoff service, sailings to St Malo continued to be operated from both Portsmouth and, during the summer months, from Plymouth. In 1978 *Armorique* opened two further routes for Brittany Ferries, both of which took the company outside the confines of the Channel for the first time. These new services connected Plymouth with Santander in Northern Spain, and Roscoff with Cork in the Irish Republic. This operation involved one ship in a complex schedule linking four countries by running Plymouth-Santander-Plymouth-Roscoff-Cork-Roscoff-Plymouth.

Rapid expansion now turned what had begun less than ten years earlier as a very modest attempt to ship French vegetables to England into a major European ferry business. This growth, however, severely stretched Brittany Ferries' resources and in 1981 heavy losses threatened to bankrupt the company. A rescue package was mounted by French banking interests, establishing the line on a firmer financial footing and securing its future for further development.

Traffic levels increased steadily on all of the company's routes and larger ships were needed. The 7,950-ton *Quiberon*, originally built in 1975 as the Swedish ferry *Nils Dacke*, was refitted with upgraded accommodation to carry 1,040 passengers and 252 cars, and joined the fleet in 1982. Still in service with Brittany Ferries, her facilities include the now usual shops, bars, lounges and restaurants, a Coffee Shop, children's playroom, two cinemas, and passenger lifts.

Brittany Ferries was not, however, the only company to be establishing new routes and introducing new ships between England and France. Two new 'super Vikings', *Viking Venturer* and *Viking Valiant*, entered service on Townsend Thoresen's Southampton routes in 1974 and 1975.

The following year Portsmouth City Council opened its new Continental Ferry Terminal in Portsmouth Harbour, which had hitherto, apart from Isle of Wight and coastal shipping services, been almost entirely the province of the Royal Navy. The benefits of Portsmouth over Southampton soon became apparent. Almost an hour's sailing time could be saved on cross-Channel services, which meant less fuel consumed and a more effective utilisation of ships. Townsend Thoresen began operating *Viking I* from Portsmouth, renaming her *Viking Victory* in honour of the city, home of Nelson's famous flagship. (Some years later her sister, the former Thoresen vessel *Viking II*, was purchased by Sealink and renamed *Earl William* to commence a new service from Portsmouth to the Channel Islands.) Over the next ten years all of Townsend Thoresen's Southampton services were transferred to Portsmouth.

In 1976 P&O Normandy Ferries, operators of *Dragon* and *Leopard* between Southampton and Le Havre, opened a new service from Dover to Boulogne, competing with Sealink and with Townsend Thoresen's adjacent route between Dover and Calais. In all probability this new route was only initiated because the line's owners, P&O, whose subsidiary companies operated several ferry routes around Britain, simply had a spare vessel. This was the *Lion*, built in 1976 for Burns & Liard's Irish Sea service between Ardrossen and Belfast. She was moved south to inaugurate the new route from Dover in the spring of 1976, making up to four return crossings a day. Capacity was later increased when Normandy Ferries purchased two 1972-built Scandinavian vessels. They entered service at Dover, renamed *Tiger* and *Panther*, in 1978 and 1980 respectively. From the beginning of the 1980s the company dropped the Normandy label, becoming simply P&O Ferries.

Townsend Thoresen, having established a lead in the operation of car-ferry services from Dover with the development of its 'Free Enterprise' fleet, the latest of which, *Free Enterprise VIII*, had been launched in 1974, introduced a trio of revolutionary new ships in the early 1980s for what they called their 'Blue Riband Service' between Dover and Calais. These large (6,500 tons) and powerful German-built ships, *Spirit of Free Enterprise*, *Herald of Free Enterprise* and *Pride of Free Enterprise*, brought superior standards and faster crossings to the Channel. In her first year *Herald of Free Enterprise*, which was to become notorious later for other reasons, made a record crossing between the pier-heads of Dover and Calais in 52 min 53 sec, at an average speed of 24.7 knots, although scheduled berth-to-berth crossing times were maintained at 75 minutes.

A new cross-Channel route was opened in the mid-1970s by the Danish company Olau Line (a name contracted from that of its founder, Ole Lauritzen). This ran between Sheerness, in North Kent, and Dunkirk, and was in addition to the Olau Line service already operating from the Kent port to Vlissingen (Flushing) in Holland. Although the Vlissingen service remained successful for a number of years, the link with France was short-lived.

In 1980 and 1981 Sealink UK began its 'Flagship Service' from Dover with two new 7,000-ton Belfast-built vessels *St Anselm* (named after an 11th-century Archbishop of Canterbury) and *St Christopher* (patron saint of wayfarers and, latterly, of motorists). Sealink's French partners SNCF introduced the even larger 9,000-ton twins *Côte d'Azur* and *Champs Elysées*. On the Ostend route the Belgian operator RMT had introduced three new ferries since 1975, *Prinses Maria-Esmeralda*, *Princesse Marie-Christine* and *Prins Albert*, and in 1982 chartered the Swedish vessel *Stena Nautica*, which it later purchased outright and renamed *Reine Astrid*.

Within the space of just a few years the style and spaciousness of car-ferries sailing on the short-sea routes had been transformed, and competition between the private

Above right Ostend was always a busy and fascinating port, with the large fleet of the Belgian state-owned ferry company RMT, which for well over a hundred years operated services from here to Dover, and in its final years to Ramsgate. Its vessels were always smart but, sadly, its operation became increasingly uneconomic.

Right As passengers transfer at Ostend from the car and passenger ferry *Prins Albert*, which has just arrived on an afternoon sailing from England in 1985, a locomotive of the Belgian State Railways waits to haul the Tauern Express, composed mainly of sleeping cars, on through Brussels and as far as the German border, on the first part of the train's long journey to Southern Germany and Austria.

The entrance to the car-ferry terminal at Dover's Eastern Docks, with the Jubilee Way, which provides direct access to the A2, sweeping across the terminal from the cliffs on the left. When this view was taken shortly after the Jubilee Way opened in 1977, there were passenger car-ferry services from here to Boulogne, Calais, Dunkirk, Ostend and Zeebrugge. Today Calais is the only destination (other than for freight, for which services are also run to Zeebrugge), but traffic volumes and passenger numbers passing through the terminal have increased significantly.

operators and the nationalised concerns was becoming ever more fierce. Road access to Dover's Eastern Docks was much improved in 1977 with the opening of the Jubilee Way, an extension of the A2, which completely bypasses the town. The new road sweeps out from the cliffs on an elevated section above the docks, giving motorists a sudden and dramatic view of Dover Harbour as it curves down towards the terminal entrance.

A little further north along the Kent coast the Thanet town of Ramsgate, which had been considered and rejected as a cross-Channel port in the 1860s, was now to have another chance. Its Royal Harbour, originally constructed in the 18th century to provide a safe haven for vessels in the vicinity of the treacherous Goodwin Sands, had been granted its title by George IV to become the only Royal harbour in Britain. During the 1970s it developed into a major centre for importing foreign-built cars into Britain, principally Volkswagens.

A business group was formed to start a new vehicle and passenger service between Ramsgate and Dunkirk West, the new harbour development at Gravelines between Dunkirk and Calais. This new service, styled Dunkerque-Ramsgate Ferries, operated during the summer of 1980, using the vessel *Nuits Saint Georges*, which sailed from an exposed ferry-berth constructed by Thanet District Council outside Ramsgate's harbour wall. It was not, however, a success - in fact, it was a disaster! The exposed position made docking at Ramsgate difficult in high winds, severe silting problems required the constant

attentions of a dredger to clear the approaches to the berth, and on one occasion the ship ran aground for 3 hours. The subsequent blockading of Dunkirk by French fishermen over a fisheries dispute caused further disruption to schedules, but the venture itself was underfinanced, and culminated in the abandonment of the service with the arrest of *Nuits Saint Georges* in Dunkirk for unpaid debts. The hopes of the local people of Ramsgate to revitalise their Regency town, which had been in decline for some time, now seemed to be dashed.

However, help was to come from an unexpected and rather distant quarter. Rederi AB Sally, Finland's largest privately owned shipping company and operator of ferries across the Baltic Sea, was seeking to expand its interests elsewhere in Europe. The demise of the short-lived Ramsgate-Dunkirk service seemed to provide just the opportunity for entering the lucrative cross-Channel market on the short-sea route, the most intensive network of ferry services in the world, provided that facilities at Ramsgate could be improved. Negotiations with the local

MARITIME HERITAGE

Council to re-open the route from Ramsgate resulted in a joint agreement whereby Sally Line Ltd, a wholly owned subsidiary of Rederi AB Sally, would provide an investment of £5 million for initial development at the ferry terminal, in return for a 99-year lease on the use of what has become known as Port Ramsgate. One of the company's Baltic Sea vessels, the 5,300-ton *Viking 5*, was renamed *The Viking* and brought over to inaugurate the new 2½-hour crossing in June 1981. Unfortunately, later in the summer she developed engine trouble and had to be quickly replaced by a chartered ship. But unlike the previous year, the route demonstrated its appeal and potential, although continuing difficulties at Ramsgate underlined the urgent need for considerable harbour development work if the port was to be established as the permanent base for a year-round ferry operation.

Sally Line's French terminal is located at Dunkirk West. Although this is a development of the Port of Dunkirk Authority, the town of Dunkirk itself is situated several kilometres east of the ferry-berth. However, road connections are good, and in addition the company has recognised the benefits of encouraging shop-seeking day-trippers to the route, laying on a bus service linking the town centre and the hypermarket with its sailings from Ramsgate. Train connections are also available from Dunkirk town station to Paris (Nord).

Following the experience of Sally Line's first year at Ramsgate, further negotiations between the shipping company and Thanet District Council resulted in an agreement whereby the Council would undertake a dredging programme to deepen the approach channel and provide a turning area adjacent to the berth, while Sally Line would build an outer breakwater to enclose and protect the berth. This effectively formed a third, or outer-outer harbour, since Ramsgate already had an existing inner and outer harbour. To ensure the success of this engineering work, the port's tidal flows were studied by a research group at Helsinki University. The dredging work needed to be largely finished before the service, which had now been suspended, was able to recommence in 1982, although the extensive harbour construction, including the building of additional ferry-berths for freight operation, was to take several years before it was finally completed, and adverse weather would no longer be a cause of disrupted schedules.

A two-ship operation began, enabling more frequent sailings between the two ports, and *Prinsessan Desiree* (5,700 gross tons) was chartered to augment the service. During the following years a succession of other ships were used on the route, all with the characteristic red hull bearing the legend 'Sally Viking Line'. Following changes in the company's Baltic Sea operations, the 'Viking' connection was dropped in 1985, the naming nomenclature of their English Channel ships was changed, and the service was promoted as 'Sally Line', its ferries often being referred to by Kent locals simply as 'the Sally'. On board the vessels special facilities were included for young children, and live music was provided on some crossings. With a simple, competitive fare structure, attractive ships and Scandinavian smorgasbord a feature of every sailing, Sally Line quickly established itself as a welcome and distinctive newcomer to the Channel. Furthermore, cross-Channel trade was booming generally, and Sally's success did not seem to be at the expense of other operators from nearby Dover.

The new breakwater at Ramsgate, together with major civil engineering works to reclaim land on the West Rocks, below the cliffs, and to provide parking and marshalling areas, was eventually completed in 1986. In the same year Sally Line introduced *Viking 2* (not to be confused with Thoresen's vessel of a similar name), which it claimed to be the most luxurious craft running between England and France. After a hesitant start, Ramsgate had joined the ranks of England's Continental gateways.

Like most Channel ferry ports, Ramsgate is claimed to have easy access to the country's trunk road network. Certainly, the road link between the town and the M2 has been considerably improved, but one startling restriction is the necessity for cross-Channel traffic, large commercial vehicles included, to negotiate the town's streets, including a right-angle bend on the cliff-top above the harbour, and a 180-degree turn to enter the long, winding road along the harbour's edge to the ferry terminal. Attempts to run a new direct road to the harbour from the west of the town along the base of the cliffs have met with considerable opposition. More recent proposals to run an access road through a tunnel in the cliffs and thence via a causeway to the ferry terminal may prove to be more successful. These new plans also envisage considerable development of the West Rocks site, with offices, shopping facilities and even an hotel.

Major changes were to occur on the Channel, and on other UK ferry routes, by the transfer of ownership of the ferry fleet of British Railways. In comparison with the regional structure that had been created immediately after railway nationalisation, the centralised control of British-flagged Sealink ships that had been adopted in 1963 had enabled the British Railways Board to utilise its shipping assets more efficiently. Even so, in a fast-developing industry, the management of a large nationalised fleet was of necessity cumbersome, the process of obtaining ministerial approval for building new vessels was protracted, and the ability to respond flexibly to the pressures and opportunities of competition was somewhat inhibited. Since, in addition, an increasing proportion of the business involved the carriage of private cars and commercial freight rather than railway passengers, the Conservative Government considered that Sealink UK would prosper better in the private sector, unhindered by its traditional links with the railways. The British Sealink fleet, together with the various railway-owned harbours, was therefore offered for sale.

Several concerns expressed interest although, for monopoly reasons, the Government ruled out bids from existing major cross-Channel ferry operators. As with most privatisations, there were discontented mumblings that the rules were unfair and that the price eventually accepted was too low. One of the big contenders and a potential winner had been Trafalgar House, owner of Cunard Line. The company subsequently withdrew, and in 1985 Sealink was sold, for £66 million, to Sea Containers, the Bermuda-based but American-owned international container-leasing business. A UK subsidiary company was formed to run the newly established

Sealink British Ferries, headed by one of SeaCo's founders, the American James Sherwood. His aim was to enlarge the company, modernise the fleet, and to increase turnover by placing a major emphasis on passenger service.

One of the first moves of Sealink's new owners was to substantially upgrade the ferry services running from both Weymouth and Portsmouth to the Channel Islands. This was done by refurbishing the *Earl William* (formerly Thoresen's ferry *Viking II*) and the more recently introduced *Earl Granville* (formerly Sally's Baltic ferry *Viking 4*). Fares were also increased in line with the new facilities provided, but this strategy, on what is basically an economy tourist route, did not meet with success.

At much the same time a new ferry company was being formed by the creation of Channel Island Ferries, a joint venture between Brittany Ferries and Huelin Renouf, a Jersey-based concern. The Brittany Ferries' vessel *Benodet*, renamed *Corbiere*, was transferred to the new route from Portsmouth in direct competition with Sealink. After winning a substantial proportion of the total Channel Islands traffic by offering more competitive fares, a combined operation between Sealink and CIF, called British Channel Island Ferries, was established to run joint services from both Portsmouth and Weymouth. Sealink's involvement in this arrangement was, however, short-lived, and following an industrial dispute over the issue it withdrew from the enterprise and from all Channel Island sailings. Soon afterwards Sealink also abandoned its Weymouth-Cherbourg services.

British Channel Island Ferries remained the sole operator to the Channel Islands. In 1989 it transferred all its operations to Poole and introduced a new ship, *Rozel* (originally the British Railways ferry *St Edmund* from the Harwich-Hook of Holland route), which, at almost 9,000 tons, was the largest ship ever to serve the Channel Islands. The company also acquired the smaller *Havelet*. *Rozel* was later replaced at Poole by *Beauport*, a ship that had already experienced a varied career, including service for Brittany Ferries as both *Prince of Brittany* and *Reine Mathilde*, since being originally built as *Prince of Fundy* in 1970 for service in North America.

Later attempts by smaller operators to revive ferry services to the Channel Islands from Weymouth have not been successful, although BCIF, bought out by Condor in 1994, transferred *Havelet* to Weymouth. But with the emphasis of this route now very much on high-speed ferries, and with services transferred back to Poole, the once familiar 'Channel Island boats' are no longer seen at Weymouth Quay.

The Dorset town of Poole, its quay, and its small commercial port, lie at the head of Poole Harbour, a large though mostly shallow area of enclosed water dotted with islands, and beautifully situated close to the Purbeck Hills. The natural harbour has a narrow entrance to the sea at Sandbanks, across which operates a chain-ferry for vehicles using the road between Bournemouth and Swanage, saving the much longer journey around the north of the harbour through Wareham. In the 18th century Poole had developed important links with Newfoundland, and was later involved in the coastal trade in clay, which was shipped

from here to the potteries in the North of England. The town's largely 19th-century waterfront is a particularly interesting area. But with its picturesque setting and its holiday atmosphere, Poole seems at first an odd choice for a major ferry terminal. Nevertheless, freight services to Cherbourg had been operated from here by Truckline since 1973, its ships carefully negotiating the narrow channel that winds its way from the harbour entrance, past Brownsea Island, and on towards the town itself. In 1984 Truckline was purchased by Brittany Ferries, which expanded the service and introduced passenger sailings on the route. The Truckline name was retained, and a successful economy approach used, offering a basic, value-for-money service based on the well-established network of les Routiers French roadside restaurants. The first vessel employed on this service following the takeover was *Cornouailles* (later to become *Havelet* and transferred to British Channel Island Ferries).

Two years later Brittany Ferries expanded further by opening a new route from Portsmouth to Ouistreham, a small resort and international yachting harbour at the mouth of the River Orne and 10 kilometres from Caen, Normandy's most important city. A new ship, the former Dutch ferry *Prinses Beatrix*, was acquired for this service, and was completely and magnificently refurbished in French style and given the new name *Duc de Normandie*. The Portsmouth-Ouistreham route (although in fact the French destination is called Caen in the company's brochures) has rapidly developed to become Brittany Ferries' major cross-Channel link.

At Newhaven, the jointly operated Sealink service to Dieppe had, after initial success following the introduction of car-ferries, begun to gain something of a reputation for unreliability, much of this due to industrial action on the French side. In 1985 the new owners of Sealink British Ferries withdrew from this route, leaving its operation in the hands of the French. The service was renamed Sealink Dieppe Ferries and new ships were soon introduced, first *Versailles* (ex-*Stena Nautica*) and later *Champs Elysées* (transferred from the Dover-Calais route). But unreliable operation arising from continuing industrial unrest amongst the French crews remained a feature of the route.

Soon after the privatisation of Sealink UK, the Belgian ferry operator RMT, which had been a member of the international Sealink trading consortium, decided to withdraw its Ostend-based fleet from this scheme, and in 1986 concluded a marketing agreement with Townsend Thoresen, which would henceforth handle promotion and bookings in Britain for the Dover-Ostend service. The Belgian ships were repainted with orange Townsend Thoresen hulls, but retained their own funnel markings. At the same time RMT took steps to prevent Sealink British Ferries from operating its own competing service between Dover and Ostend (which had recently started, using *St David*, transferred from the Irish Sea) and an acrimonious dispute ensued. This had the rather unfortunate consequence that Belgian ships were no longer permitted to use the Admiralty Pier ferry-berth at Dover, which was operated by Sealink and enabled car-ferry sailings to handle railway passengers from the adjacent station. This meant that those sailings to Ostend intended to connect with boat-trains from London had first to load cars at the car-ferry terminal in the Eastern Docks, move across the harbour to a conventional berth at the Admiralty Pier to pick up railway passengers, then sail on to Ostend. This manoeuvre, which took place in reverse on all in-bound rail-connected sailings, added 45 minutes to the total crossing time for car passengers, who must have wondered what it was all about. Clearly, competition did not always operate in the passengers' best interest!

During the mid-1980s both RMT and Townsend Thoresen enlarged several of their older car-ferries. This rather drastic shipyard operation was carried out by lengthening the hull with the insertion of a new mid-section or by adding extra decks beneath the original superstructure. Sometimes both were done. The result of these alterations was to provide considerably increased vehicle capacity and greater passenger space in line with more recently built ferries, but in almost every case it significantly spoiled the external appearance of the vessels.

Other changes, too, were happening on the Channel. In 1985 European Ferries, the owners of Townsend Thoresen, purchased from P&O the former fleet of Normandy Ferries, which operated routes from Southampton to Le Havre and from Dover to Boulogne. P&O's ferry division had not significantly modernised its ships nor upgraded its services to keep pace with that of its competitors, so the parent P&O Group seemed happy to withdraw from the Channel and to concentrate on its other shipping operations, on managing its international property portfolio, and on building Bovis Homes, all part of P&O's extensive business interests. The P&O Ferries' fleet was integrated into Townsend Thoresen's existing operations. The Southampton-based *Dragon* and *Leopard* were moved to Portsmouth, ending the former port's long association with cross-Channel passenger sailings, but both ships were withdrawn the following year, *Dragon* being transferred to the Irish Sea and *Leopard* being sold. But the disappearance of the famed P&O name from cross-Channel services was, in the event, to be brief.

By 1986, in spite of these additions to its fleet and the launching in September of the first of its new 26,000-ton superferries, *Pride of Dover*, Townsend Thoresen's parent company, the European Ferries Group, operator of ferry services from several ports around the British Isles, was in serious danger of collapse. Keith Wickenden, the company's charismatic Chairman and the doyen of the UK ferry industry, had died in an accident a few years previously,

A scene at Dover's car-ferry terminal in 1985. On the left, at number 4 berth, is the Belgian ferry *Prinses Maria-Esmeralda*, showing how she has been enlarged by raising the superstructure and adding further vehicle decks. Sponsons (air-filled tanks at waterline level) have been added along the hull to maintain the stability of the now larger ship. On the far right, at berth number 6, is the French vessel *Côte d'Azur*. In the centre, at berth number 5, is the Townsend Thoresen ferry *Herald of Free Enterprise*. During her first few months of service she set a new Channel record by crossing between the pier-heads of Dover and Calais in under 53 minutes. In March 1987, however, she was to set out on a cross-Channel voyage from Zeebrugge that she was never to complete.

MARITIME HERITAGE

Above left The third of Townsend Thoresen's new ships was *Pride of Free Enterprise*, here seen at Dover in 1984. Behind her is the funnel of the French ferry *Côte d'Azur*.

Below left With its new 'Spirit' Class ships, Townsend Thoresen was able to offer more frequent sailings and faster crossings on what it called its 'Blue Riband Service' between Dover and Calais.

Above British Rail's new 'Saint' Class ferry *St Christopher*, introduced on Sealink's services from Dover in 1981.

Below St Anselm, introduced in 1980, entering Boulogne in the new livery of Sealink British Ferries, which was adopted to give the fleet a new identity separate from that of British Rail prior to the 1985 privatisation of Sealink UK.

announced the imminent closure of its Dover-Boulogne link. Although SeaCats continue to operate to Boulogne from Folkestone, there was considerable concern in Boulogne, a traditional cross-Channel ferry port that had always been a popular destination with British day-trippers, at the huge loss of trade to Calais.

P&O's *Pride of Kent* (ex-*Spirit of Free Enterprise*) was lengthened and her capacity increased to carry 1,800 passengers and 475 cars. In addition, a freight-ferry, which had been under construction for the company, was instead completed as a major new passenger vessel, becoming the 28,500-ton *Pride of Burgundy*. With five vessels on the Dover-Calais route, P&O was now able to offer departures every 45 minutes from each port at peak periods. A new theme based on P&O's historic liner past was adopted in the smart, on-board decor (with Peninsular lounges and POSH bars) and also extensively used in the company's marketing. At both Dover and Calais, new computerised booking and 'open loading' arrangements were introduced, considerably speeding up the processing of passengers and their cars, allowing vehicles arriving at the terminal to stop just once before driving straight on to the next available ferry, where all bars and catering facilities would be open. A similar scheme was introduced by Stena Sealink.

At both Dover and Calais, considerable investment in improved port facilities continued. Dover opened its seventh ro-ro ferry-berth at the Eastern Docks, which over the years has been considerably expanded by the Dover Harbour Board on land reclaimed from the harbour. The 24-hour movement of shipping in the harbour and the flow of up to 1,000 vehicles an hour through the terminal complex, the busiest in Europe, is overseen from a control centre overlooking the docks. At Calais, where the port has been greatly extended under the management of Calais Chamber of Commerce to become Europe's largest car-ferry terminal, a wider harbour entrance has been created to enable incoming and outgoing vessels to pass each other within the confines of the port. An eighth ferry-berth was opened at Calais in 1995.

Changes in customs regulations were introduced within the European Community, increasing the allowance for duty-free goods purchased on board the ferries, and almost totally eliminating controls on the import of alcohol and other commodities purchased, tax paid, in another member state. The considerably lower tax on these goods in France has stimulated an increase in British day-trip passengers on the shorter routes (some sailings becoming known as 'booze cruises', as whole van-loads of beer and wine, for 'personal consumption', are regularly shipped back from France). British supermarket chains such as Sainsbury and Tesco were not slow to set up shop in Calais to benefit from this trade. Ferry operators themselves make considerable additional revenue from on-board sales of duty-free goods. Indeed, this income helps to subsidise fares, and the threat that these concessions will be withdrawn as internal borders within the Community are abolished gives them serious cause for concern.

The Belgian RMT became known as the Oostende-Dover Line from 1991, and established a new corporate identity for its fleet, with the company's name and a new logo appearing on its ships. In 1992, after a considerable delay in construction and long disputes with her builders in Antwerp, the Line introduced the magnificent *Prins Filip*, bringing impressive new standards to its route between Dover and Ostend. Almost 29,000 tons, she was equipped with advanced navigational and safety equipment, and had a luxuriously furnished interior designed to cruise-ship standards, incorporating two large bars, two cinemas, and both waiter-service and self-service restaurants. She also had well-equipped cabin accommodation located forward, away from the main passenger areas, for the benefit of those wishing for a quiet rest on overnight crossings.

The entry into service of the huge *Prins Filip* required a new berth at Ostend and the deepening of the access channels to the port. There were later problems with her massive bulk at Dover when, after being blown against a pier, she needed two tugs to hold her alongside the berth against the force of a south-westerly gale while she unloaded.

The Line's new identity did not remain unchanged for long. Towards the end of 1993 it was announced that the Belgian company did not intend to renew its marketing agreement with P&O, but had instead concluded a deal with Sally Line. With effect from the following January, RMT became known simply as Oostende Lines, transferring all its Ostend services, including Jetfoil operations, from Dover to Sally's base at Ramsgate. With the move to Ramsgate, car-ferry services to Ostend were operated by *Prins Filip*, together with the refurbished vessels *Reine Astrid* and *Prins Albert*. Considerable new investment in port facilities was needed at Ramsgate, in particular further dredging of the harbour to accommodate *Prins Filip*, which completely dominated the harbour area when in port. The first year of service at Ramsgate was marred, however, when an enclosed passenger walkway to the *Prins Filip* collapsed, killing six people.

Further west, the Newhaven-Dieppe crossing had been entirely in French hands since 1985. In 1992 the operators, SNAT, announced heavy losses and plans to terminate the route. True to form, French industrial action in response to this announcement succeeded in closing the route earlier than had been planned. However, several other operators expressed interest in this crossing, and the service was taken over by Stena Sealink, refurbishing the ships and giving them new names, *Stena Parisien* (formerly *Champs Elysées*) and *Stena Londoner* (formerly *Versailles*, and previously a Stena Line ship). The link was dubbed the 'Capital Cities Route' because of its central location on a direct line joining London and Paris. An impressive new terminal was opened at Dieppe, right at the harbour entrance, saving 25 minutes on the crossing from Newhaven. This change meant, however, that the ferries no longer arrived among the cafés and bistros of the old harbour, from where their comings and goings could be observed in comfort from a quayside table.

In the western Channel, where the effects of the tunnel are less keenly felt, the mood has been even more confident as huge new vessels have entered service. Nowhere is this more evident than at Portsmouth, where the much enlarged though often congested Continental Ferry Port handled more large ferries (those over 20,000 tons) than

RMT's *Princesse Marie-Christine* approaches Ramsgate Harbour in 1995 following the previous year's transfer of Ostend services there from Dover to be operated in collaboration with Sally Line's sailings to Dunkirk.

any other single facility in the world. The sight of these massive vessels, towering over the surrounding buildings and other shipping as they appear to squeeze through the narrow entrance of the harbour, with an Admiralty tug on standby, is quite amazing. The terminal's owners, Portsmouth City Council, doubtless as surprised as anyone over this success, have been seeking private buyers able to continue with the heavy programme of investment required.

In 1989 Brittany Ferries introduced the French-built, 23,000-ton *Bretagne* on its route from Portsmouth to St Malo, also operating her on sailings to Spain. The Finnish-built 27,000-ton *Normandie* joined *Duc de Normandie* in 1992 on the Caen (Ouistreham) service. Magnificent vessels, looking more like modern cruise-liners than cross-Channel car-ferries, they incorporate an extensive range of high-quality accommodation and facilities. The standard of catering on board Brittany Ferries' ships, endorsed by Egon Ronay, is especially highly regarded. Even in the self-service restaurants your food, having been selected and paid for, is brought to your table freshly cooked. A particular feature on most Brittany Ferries' ships is the Vienoiserie, serving a rich selection of pastries freshly prepared on board.

In spite of the great increase in size of the vessels that have been introduced by most operators in recent years, and of the lavishness of the surroundings, on busy sailings at peak periods they can still seem uncomfortably full. Passengers may have to queue to reach the bar or obtain a seat in the restaurant, and the old concept of a crowded Channel ferry, brimming over with a mass of humanity, is not yet, it seems, completely dead. On several routes, too, there have been complaints that, on off-peak sailings, some of the on-board facilities, however superb they may be, remain stubbornly closed.

P&O European Ferries, like its rivals Brittany, also introduced massive new ships at Portsmouth. The first of these, originally built as *Olympia* for Swedish owners for operation across the Baltic, is now on long-term charter to P&O as *Pride of Bilbao*. At 37,000 tons, she is the largest ferry serving any UK port, and was acquired by P&O in 1993 to inaugurate a new route from Portsmouth to Bilbao, in Spain. She warrants inclusion here as she has also operated weekend sailings on P&O's cross-Channel services between Portsmouth and Le Havre. Her internal layout has been considerably altered to meet P&O's requirements, and her range of on-board facilities is impressive, with an extensive range of cabin accommodation. She has been extremely successful in attracting passengers, many of whom simply book for the round voyage to Spain, enjoying a sea-travel experience in traditional P&O style.

Two other large vessels joined P&O's Portsmouth-based fleet quite unexpectedly. Olau Line, which had operated a highly regarded North Sea service between Sheerness and Vlissingen for 20 years, had been trying to introduce cost-cutting measures on this route, but was unable to reach agreement with the German seafarers' union. Suddenly, in early 1994, the company announced that this service would close. Immediately P&O entered discussions with the owners in an attempt to acquire the two recently built, 33,000-ton cruise-ferries used on this service, *Olau Britannia* and *Olau Hollandia*. In what was a great blow for users of this popular route between Britain and the Netherlands, and these included road hauliers as

MARITIME HERITAGE

Above left The shape of recent ferries can lack the graceful lines of earlier vessels! Here the rectangular *Reine Astrid*, the two stern loading doors on her massive vehicle decks clearly visible, pulls away from her berth at Dover at the commencement of a crossing to Ostend in 1994. Built in 1975, *Reine Astrid* was originally chartered by RMT from Stena Line in 1982 as *Stena Nautica*. She was later purchased outright by the Belgian company and given her new name.

Below left From an earlier position of running perhaps the most elegant of cross-Channel fleets, the Ostend service had in more recent years become distinctly second-rate. This all changed in 1992 with the introduction into service, initially from Dover but later from Ramsgate, of the magnificent *Prins Filip*, seen here departing from Ramsgate in 1994. Sadly, and in spite of its splendid new vessel, the state-owned Belgian ferry company, established in 1846 and becoming the longest surviving cross-Channel operator, was facing mounting and unsustainable losses, and in 1997 was finally forced to cease trading with the sale of all its assets, including *Prins Filip*.

Above Brittany Ferries' *Bretagne* approaches Portsmouth in 1993, followed by an Isle of Wight ferry turning behind her. Designed in Finland, model-tested in the Netherlands, and built in France under contracts drawn up by her French owners under English law, *Bretagne*, which entered service at Plymouth in 1989, demonstrates the increasingly international nature of modern shipbuilding. With a wide variety of passenger amenities that include a choice of restaurants, cafés, a coffee shop, a tea shop and several bars, she was designed to bring cruise-ship standards to an English Channel crossing.

Below left and right Extending further the modern concept of the cruise-ferry, Brittany Ferries' *Normandie* enters Portsmouth Harbour on arrival from Ouistreham, also in 1993. Many features of her design are unseen by passengers; these include the ship's advanced propulsion machinery and navigational equipment, and the containerised delivery system for the vast quantity of stores needed by a vessel carrying over 2,000 passengers. To ensure a fast turn-round in port, these containers are simply lowered by the ship's crane into a hatch from where they can be distributed around the ship while the vessel is at sea. Many of these supplies represent the duty-free goods that are sold on board, and which can account for over 10 per cent of the ship's revenue.

Above The massive *Pride of Bilbao* appears to squeeze through the narrow entrance to Portsmouth Harbour, dwarfing the fortifications of the Old Town that were originally designed to look down on threatening ships! Although mainly serving on P&O Ferries' service from Portsmouth to Spain, *Pride of Bilbao* also operates occasional sailings across the Channel.

Below Outward bound is *Pride of Le Havre*, another of several 'superferries' operating from Portsmouth's Continental Ferry Terminal on the 'central corridor' route across the Channel to France. *Pride of Le Havre*, together with her sister-ship *Pride of Portsmouth*, was acquired from Olau Line in 1994 following the ending of that company's services between Sheerness and Vlissingen, in Holland. These 33,000-ton ships had previously carried the names *Olau Hollandia* and *Olau Britannia*.

Above right *Barfleur* was introduced on to Brittany Ferries' Truckline Ferries service between Poole and Cherbourg in 1992, and is seen here in the following year berthed in Poole Harbour. Designed to undertake four crossings every 24 hours, like most ferries operating in the Western Channel she has considerable cabin accommodation for night sailings, and is also intended to carry a considerable proportion of road freight.

Right *Stena Invicta*, in the Stena Line livery adopted for English Channel services in 1996, turns in the harbour off Dover's Eastern Docks on arrival from Calais. On the right is the P&O freight-ferry *European Highway*, while in the foreground the Stena Line SeaCat *Stena Lynx III* is unloading cars.

A summer's evening departure from Ostend on board *Prins Filip*.

MARITIME HERITAGE

'FAMILY TREE' OF FERRY OPERATING COMPANIES

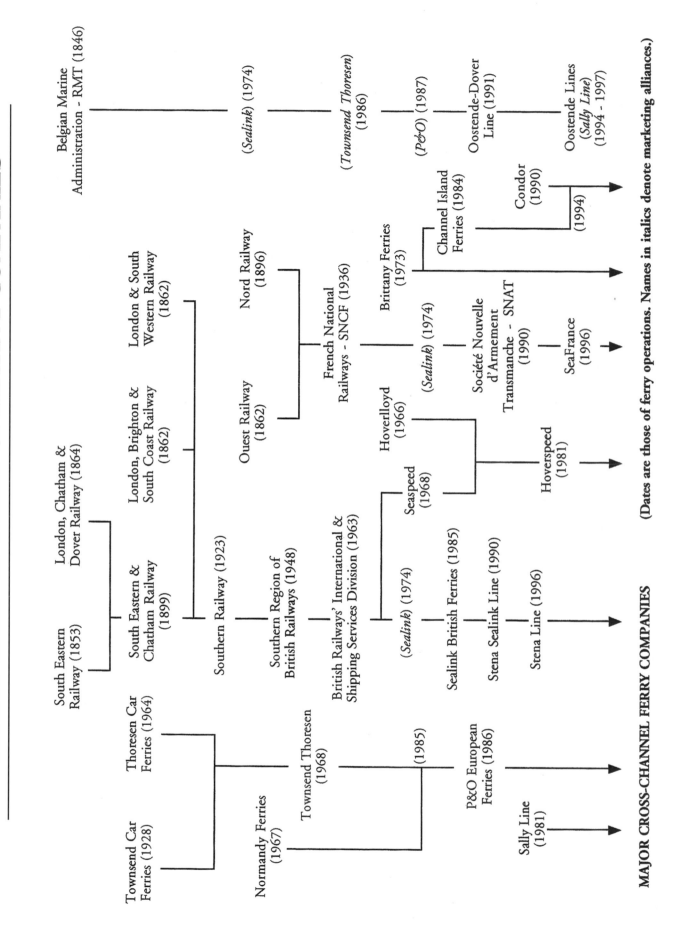

Belgian Marine Administration - RMT (1846)

(Sealink) (1974)

(Townsend Thoresen) (1986)

(P&O) (1987)

Oostende-Dover Line (1991)

Oostende Lines (Sally Line) (1994 - 1997)

London, Chatham & Dover Railway (1864)

London & South Western Railway (1862)

London, Brighton & South Coast Railway (1862)

Nord Railway (1896)

Ouest Railway (1862)

French National Railways - SNCF (1936)

Brittany Ferries (1973)

Channel Island Ferries (1984)

Condor (1990)

(1994)

(Sealink) (1974)

Société Nouvelle d'Armement Transmanche - SNAT (1990)

SeaFrance (1996)

South Eastern Railway (1853)

South Eastern & Chatham Railway (1899)

Southern Railway (1923)

Southern Region of British Railways (1948)

British Railways' International & Shipping Services Division (1963)

Hoverlloyd (1966)

Seaspeed (1968)

Hoverspeed (1981)

(Sealink) (1974)

Sealink British Ferries (1985)

Stena Sealink Line (1990)

Stena Line (1996)

Thoresen Car Ferries (1964)

Townsend Car Ferries (1928)

Normandy Ferries (1967)

Townsend Thoresen (1968)

(1985)

P&O European Ferries (1986)

Sally Line (1981)

MAJOR CROSS-CHANNEL FERRY COMPANIES

(Dates are those of ferry operations. Names in italics denote marketing alliances.)

INDEX